DANGEROUS LIAISONS
COMPLETE ORIGINAL CONCEPT

LYRICS
JOHNATHAN DANIEL STEPPE

MUSIC
MALCOLM CALUORI

DANGEROUS LIAISONS

LIBRETTO

ORIGINAL VERSION

Based on the Complete Original Concept Recording

Melpomene Music Publications
ATLANTA

Dangerous Liaisons Libretto
(Complete Original Concept)

Book design, cover design and artwork by Malcolm Caluori

All music and lyrics (BMI), copyright © 2000 Melpomene Music Group, except Intermedio Copyright © 2007, 2011 Melpomene Music Group. Music by Malcolm Caluori; Lyrics by Johnathan Daniel Steppe

First Edition
Copyright © 2016 Melpomene Music Group
All rights reserved

Published in the U.S.A. International copyright secured.

ISBN-13:   978-0692804513
ISBN-10:   069280451X

Except for brief passages quoted in newspaper, magazine, radio, television or internet reviews, no part of this book may be reproduced in any form or by any means, electronic or mechanical, including photocopying or recording, or by an information storage and retrieval system, without permission in writing from the publisher.

Melpomene Music Publications is a division of
Melpomene Music Group, Atlanta, GA. The note sphere logo
is a trademark of Melpomene Music Group.

Contents

Foreword *by Johnathan Daniel Steppe* … vii
Preface to this Edition … ix
Killing Valmont (excerpts) *by D. Hector Francis* … xii
Creating the Music *by Malcolm Caluori* … xxvii
Characters and Original Recorded Cast … xxxiii
Synopsis … xxxv

Libretto

CD1
Prologue: "The Vow"
    1.1 "Andiamo udire il mare" … 3
    1.2 At the Opera … 3
    1.3 Volanges' Supper Party … 10
    1.4 The Vow … 12

Act I–Part 1
    1.5 Prelude … 14
    1.6 Correspondences 1 … 14
    1.7 Something More Than Love … 20
    1.8 "So, how can you refuse my command?" … 21
    1.9 Madame de Tourvel … 21
    1.10 The Deal … 26
    1.11 The Chevalier Dançeny … 28
    1.12 Hunting … 31
    1.13 The Village … 33
    1.14 Incidental: "Cécile's Secret" … 34
    1.15 I Found a Letter … 34
    1.16 "Here you are at last, monsieur" … 36

1.17	Mail	37
1.18	Music Lesson	39
1.19	The Game	40
1.20	"Well, I've won again!"	41
1.21	The Plan	44
1.22	In the Garden	46
1.23	The Meeting	49
1.24	Incidental: "The Fan"	51
1.25	"Madame, we might miss the first act"	51
1.26	If Only	52

CD2

2.1	A Quandary	54
2.2	Merteuil's Recitative	58
2.3	Letters from Dançeny	58
2.4	Interlude: "Letters"	61

Act I–Part 2

2.5	If He Were Here	62
2.6	Merteuil's Success	67
2.7	Reprise: Correspondences	68
2.8	Valmont's Return	70
2.9	Confrontations	73
2.10	Interlude: "The Garden"	80
2.11	The Garden Song	81
2.12	The Fires Within	81
2.13	The Key	83
2.14	She Closes Her Eyes	87
2.15	Incidental: "Closing In"	89
2.16	The Seduction	90
2.17	A Simple Time	92
2.18	Cécile's Confession	93
2.19	Finale: Secrets	96

Intermedio
2.20 Prelude — 102
2.21 Reflections — 102
Act II
2.22 The Storm — 111
2.23 Interlude: "Tourvel's Despair" — 115
2.24 "Poor child! What is this?" — 115

CD3
3.1 The Nature of Man — 116
3.2 Interlude: "Tourvel's Departure" — 117
3.3 Valmont's Recitative — 117
3.4 Rumors — 118
3.5 Interlude: "Sunset" — 120
3.6 Seasons Running from Ourselves — 120
3.7 Forever — 121
3.8 A Heart to Run to — 123
3.9 "Victoire, you're such a villain!" — 125
3.10 The Lioness — 125
3.11 Valmont's Success — 126
3.12 "You're up awfully late this morning" — 129
3.13 Motherhood — 130
3.14 Correspondences 2 — 132
3.15 A Story — 135
3.16 "You haven't touched your supper" — 137
3.17 Speak Gently — 138
3.18 Reprise: The Game — 140
3.19 It's Not My Fault — 140
3.20 Soliloquy — 143
3.21 Promise Me Anything — 144
3.22 Tourvel's Illness — 145
3.23 The Argument — 145

3.24	Salve Regina / The Veil is Torn	150
3.25	"How long has she been here?"	152
3.26	Final Scene: Pt.1–A Paris Street	154
3.27	Final Scene: Pt.2–The Duel	158
3.28	Final Scene: Pt.3–Valmont's Words	159
3.29	Final Scene: Pt.4–When Silence Reigns	160

Recording and Chorus Credits   163

Foreword

By Johnathan Daniel Steppe

THE INITIAL DECISION to adapt *Les Liaisons Dangereuses* for the musical stage was one borne out of the impulse and enthusiasm of youth. Two friends, fresh out of high school and hungry to create, stumbled on Laclos' formidable and compelling novel. The story had all the right elements: passion, intrigue, sex and betrayal. Certainly, this would make a great musical! Yet what began as a young dream and now exists as a fully realized work, has since evolved and been tempered in the years through which the work was written. It has become not simply a derivative of a great novel, but now stands as a unique and fascinating work in its own right.

When approaching the novel for adaptation, it was crucial to me as the librettist that the work be unique. We of course wanted to remain true to Laclos, but at the same time wanted to create a musical that expanded the themes presented by Laclos, while filtering them through our own experiences and interests. I found myself drawn to the roles in which men and women were cast during the time period of the novel, and how the stratification of gender molded the characters of Valmont and the Marquise. Born into a culture which set men and women in an adversarial position to one another, the two conspirators are born into their monstrosity. Still, it is difficult to dismiss them as villains when one views the circumstances which gave them rise.

Another theme which is expanded upon in the musical is the concept of the game. *Dangerous Liaisons* is a story of intrigue, of the perilous games played between people when desires are suppressed and motives concealed. The characters of the story are extremely passionate, yet exist in a time when passions were not to be openly expressed. What happens to a person who is denied their passions? In *Dangerous Liaisons*, the characters must resort to their hidden games, games that lead to a spider web of relationships pulled taught by unspoken tensions.

With such a compelling story, endlessly complex characters, and controversial themes, it becomes immediately obvious why *Dangerous Liaisons* drew me as a writer. What might not be obvious is, why do a musical? Simply put, the natural poetry of the original work and the heightened drama intrinsic to the storyline lends itself perfectly to musicalization. The music reveals new levels to the story, expanding the audience's experience and understanding of each of the characters where simple words could not. When successful, the melding of lyric and note is magical; it transcends the mundane and gives us a greater form of storytelling.

As a lyricist, I have been blessed with not only a truly great friend, but a truly great composer with which to collaborate. What started as a dream is now a reality; where once there was nothing, there is now an exciting new musical to savor. The process of writing a musical is breathtaking, heartbreaking and nothing, yet everything, like I expected. With each word written, the work changed. Each time the work changed, I changed. My greatest wish for this work is that it will touch others the way that it has touched me. To touch others, to change them, even if subtly—that is the greatest accomplishment that any artist can achieve.

PREFACE TO THIS EDITION

A MICROPHONE. THE sheet music is open to "Speak Gently", and the brief but stirring dialogue between mother and daughter is the target. Experienced actresses originate the roles of Volanges and Cécile, and the tender moment is about to become reality. A breath; the music begins. Yearning for independence in a confusing world that has brutally defeated her pride, Cécile's voice breaks a little in her hidden shame as she responds to her heartbroken mother's own urgency to find, instead of explanations, gentle words to offer. Tensions are precariously delicate. A few strained words provide little awkward solace to either. From beneath its containing surface, a sudden surge of emotion, a fierce hug, tears, even relief of a sort . . . then a controlled parting. But there is no Volanges, not here, only Cécile—and the microphone. Volanges' lines are scheduled for a later recording session.

Each of the principal roles for the Complete Original Concept recording of *Dangerous Liaisons* was recorded individually in this way. Through the magic of the studio, the duet and its central exchange of dialogue would be melded together in the mix. When Christy Brumfield Baggett and Kristie Krabe later listened to the mixed playback, both were delighted at the effect, and moved at hearing the dramatic scene whole. The scene's authors were the only others ever to hear that recording. There was a discrepancy between the dialogue in the score and that in the libretto. In such cases, it was the libretto that contained the most current revisions and, according to the libretto, the exchange that was recorded had been replaced with new dialogue. Touched by the result of the recording, Ms. Krabe asked with some regret if it might not be kept anyway. It may yet be preserved in a post-production archive, but the exchange had to be recorded again with Steppe's changes. Of particular interest for the final recording, owing to the length of the excerpt in question and to the fact that the dialogue is paced against an underscore, thankfully this instance was spotted while there was still time to correct it.

Although such discrepancies are familiar to theatre players, they can still be difficult to catch. Of course, concerning an "original concept" album, changes to this point were not major structural alterations, but typically adjustments to wording. Still, they replace text that the librettist rejected, and so are not to be thought insignificant or unimportant changes. Nevertheless, some changes did slip through the cracks. The "acting edition" of the libretto has since come to reflect the recording even less so, while the version of the show most readily available to the public remains that of the Complete Original Concept.

For this reason, you'll find several features that make this book special. For the fifth anniversary of the recording's release to the public, this "trade edition" of the libretto has been edited specifically to match the recorded performance (including fixing the libretto's several *ad lib* sections into text), similarly to the booklet that accompanies physical copies of the CD. With technological trends leaning ever more away from the physical toward a future of electronic distribution and consumption of music, the publication of this edition (especially in its ebook format) may further serve that future as an alternative to the CD's booklet—and, happily, to its limited space and incredibly small print.

As such, it contains extras unusual for a libretto, taken from the booklet liner notes, such as cast photos, and Malcolm Caluori's article "Creating the Music," here revised and expanded. An exciting additional commentary presents excerpts from the book *Killing Valmont—The Creation of Caluori and Steppe's Dangerous Liaisons: Process, Content and Innovations*, by D. Hector Francis.

Lastly, as reflected in the table of contents, this libretto's format is indexed to the corresponding CD track numbers, for ease of use with the recording. In many ways, *Liaisons* works exceptionally well in audio presentation. Still, more than merely assuring that you catch all the words, the libretto's stage directions guide the imagination to a fuller experience of the show.

Whether enjoying the recording, or simply cozying up for an interesting or entertaining read, this volume is the perfect *Dangerous Liaisons* companion.

Official Selections piano/vocal songbook also available. Acting Edition of the Dangerous Liaisons libretto available from the publisher for perusal and production use only.

www.DangerousLiaisonsTheMusical.com

KILLING VALMONT

The Creation of Caluori and Steppe's *Dangerous Liaisons*: Process, Content and Innovations

Excerpts from the book by D. Hector Francis

Prologue

THE PROJECT TO produce the Complete Original Concept recording of Caluori and Steppe's *Dangerous Liaisons* (what Melpomene refers to as DLOCR), was originally imagined only as a simple demo recording, though proposed with the intent that it serve multiple purposes: as a record for posterity of the complete original concept, of course, prior to any impending cuts and other dramatic revision; as a type of workshop in itself to aid in this process, presenting the whole work in context for the writers' benefit; as a single recording—or perhaps a selection of recordings—to serve as a formal 'shopable' demo for use later on. Holding a considerably broader appeal than anticipated, it suddenly flourished into quite a glorified musical theatre demo indeed, attracting interested involvement from about the nation and, in time, coming available to the world.

The periodic updates and notices that were sent out to those wishing to follow the progress of the DLOCR project as it was unfolding quickly grew to include the many people who became directly connected with the recording's realisation. Collectively, these notices, written by Malcolm Caluori in his capacity as project coordinator, form a sort of diary, chronicling the many steps, trials and emotions that came into play in bringing the project to fruition. (It is available for free at this special link: www.dldiary.com) Reading the story that this production diary tells, the excitement is palpable. There is, however, more story to be told ahead of any updates sent out, the story that took place when no one outside was yet looking. It was just two friends: Johnathan, a talented and intuitive Thespian and vocalist with a hunger to tell stories; and Malcolm, an irrepressibly creative musician who also loved the marriage of music and drama. They shared a mutual passion, together devouring newly discovered musicals, operettas, opera. Both writer and composer had experience performing on stage, and each had already had a bash or two at some ideas of his own. Johnathan, already writing for the theatre, had developed some work on a comic operetta. And as a teenager, Malcolm became so inspired by opera that he began creating one, also based on an original story, and had even conducted some of its music in concert with orchestra, soloists and chorus. And there were, at this point, thoroughly documented plans underway for a dramatic oratorio (*Crestia*), some of its choral music already in sketch. A fortuitous bond, to be sure. Only a matter of time and the quickening of a tantalising subject stood between the inevitable collaboration and the somehow still unsuspecting collaborators.

One day, having recently become aware of Laclos' story, *Les Liaisons Dangereuses*, Johnathan rang Malcolm and suggested they turn it into a musical "before someone else does," he said. Malcolm didn't know the story. But, he thought, Johnathan seemed quite sure; he was the theatre man, after all. He decided he'd have a look at the story, even though it was understood between the two of them that the idea of writing a major new work together was appealing, and that they had basically already agreed.

The first thing Caluori did was watch the 1988 Stephen Frears film, *Dangerous Liaisons* (Glenn Close, John Malkovich, Michelle Pfeiffer, et al.). Then he hesitated. He noted the expensive costumes and lavish sets, the "flowery," oh-so-formal (potentially difficult to follow) language, the complicated (potentially difficult to follow) plot that bordered on convolution spurred on by the many intertwined characters—the lot, of course, having unfamiliar (potentially difficult to follow) French names. He noted that conversion to the contemporary American musical theatre stage would have some factors to confront and solve. But he trusted Steppe's training and instincts in making the suggestion, and proceeded to the next phase. "As it turns out," Caluori now explains with a laugh, "I found out years later that Johnathan didn't know the story either. He had seen an advertisement for the movie. Not even a trailer, I think, but a print ad!" With raised finger and eyebrow he adds, "He did read the book before I ever did, though."

The story seems, in fact, a perfect candidate, already adapted multiple times each for stage, television, film, ballet, opera and radio. The Conrad Susa opera, *The Dangerous Liaisons*, premiered in San Francisco and was televised in 1994. And there is Belgian composer Piet Swerts's *Les Liaisons Dangereuses* from 1996. And although there is now the Spanish language musical *Las Relaciones Peligrosas*, which premiered in Argentina in 2012, there was no musical theatre adaptation, large or small, to be found whilst Caluori and Steppe's *Dangerous Liaisons* was being written.

Perhaps it was that list of hurdles that had discouraged earlier adaptations. An equally likely culprit, the original novel is epistolary in form, written as a collection of 174 numbered letters sent between the several characters. Caluori writes that, "the characters are not face to face and interactive scenes [have to be] fabricated." He explains that, although there are instances where a letter may describe an interaction, "the bulk of the book is presented as directly addressed conversations. The difficulty with this is that . . . one conversation may spread across a broad range of letters, and that during this conversation, significant amounts of time have elapsed and events have taken place that weave themselves into the discussions." A single scene might be built from bits of letters scattered throughout the book. And, he points out, "Once this correspondence widens to include a number of people, things become rather complicated." Unwinding this overlapping and multi-directional collection of accounts, opinions, self-aggrandisements, attacks, advice, and pleadings into a linear sequence of dramatic action is a challenging, perhaps deterring, prerequisite for potential adaptors.

Still, Steppe was right about wanting to beat the competition to the post. Shortly into DLOCR recording sessions, word came out that a musical called *The Game* was going to be opening in New York. It was written by a pair of long-time music industry professionals, and backed by some real funding. Its writers, successful in their fields, were not normally theatre writers but had pop music backgrounds, and it was quickly deduced that their version did not claim the same scale, sophistication or artistic bearing that Caluori and Steppe aspired to present. By contrast, they each had a foot in the popular world of musical theatre, and a foot in the classical arts world of opera and literature. *Liaisons*, though typically called a musical for want of a tidy category, naturally shares this ambiguity. Still, they kept a close eye on the developments surrounding *The Game*, which would meet the wider public before *Dangerous Liaisons*.

But in the beginning, there was only the quest. *Dangerous Liaisons* was not a commissioned work. A commission was never sought, and likely could not have been procured in any case. Though both collaborators were quite prolific and recognised as exceptional talents, each with celebrated achievements in both performance and writing, their young careers had not been broadly established. The work would have to be relegated to their free time, and would have no readily awaiting prospects upon its eventual completion. Neither had written a musical before; both were fortunately still green enough that their initial spark of inspiration would not be intimidated by the potentially daunting prospect of undertaking such a massive commitment without much guidance or even a plan, really. Instead, their burgeoning creativity and ever broadening expertise had both of them primed to tackle the task, to discover the way by accepting the journey.

The pair were not so entirely persuaded into institutional convention as to succumb to some of the genre's enduring, inadvertent blind spots. The path that prepared them for this juncture, and further conveyed them through the piece's writing, was deeply coloured by a conviction, by an insistent personal perspective towards music dramaturgy that rearranges traditional notions—and in due course re-evaluates entirely what musicologist Joseph Kerman refers to as, "the perennial central problem of operatic dramaturgy." That is to say, "the mutual qualification of action and music." (More precisely, "the relationship or interplay between these two," the quality of *action* characteristic of drama, and the quality of reflective, imaginative articulation characteristic of *music*.)

Having now wholly stepped into the arena of drama, the two would turn their dramatically inclined intellects to carving their path from the *inside*. In the end, that path would produce a work that involves a host of refined dramaturgic practises, and exhibits an evolution, which, despite its shortcomings—more probably, because of them—reaches a powerful reconciliation of music's introspection to drama's action through the pioneering of an unprecedented collaborative method.

This project was not destined to be a "write a libretto, then set it to music" affair. Nor, at the time, would either of them have wanted it that way. So, where to begin? Primarily, there were really only two factors with which they need concern themselves. First, the story, the creation itself, the misty vision of the drama-to-be, an assemblage of yet undefined scenes and songs (*the adaptation*). Second, the surface, the creating of the creation, the providing of the verse and the music (*the treatment*). This was no poem, skit or piano fantasia; there was a lot of work to confront, and some coordinated manner would be needed on both levels.

from Chapter One: Songs and Scenes

Thematic Continua and Constituent Forms

Whilst observing a drama presented in combination with music, one makes psychological associations between the two, as they coincide. In other words, music's own, abstract meanings become, by association, augmented with literary meaning deriving from the drama: sentiments, characters, moments, exchanges, concepts, even objects.

It works both ways, of course, and there is a correlation to the use of associative themes in literature. A broad connection that

Steppe makes, for example, is that of nature and her progression of seasons with the character and storyline of Madame de Tourvel. In his libretto, one finds the idea following Tourvel in various ways as the story plays out. Caluori, too, ties music to characters, perhaps most abundantly though to that of the Marquise, who seems to have her hand in everything. Musical reference is an important means of conveying her omnipresent influence, especially at times when she herself is not on stage.

Thematic reminiscence refers to the practise wherein prominent melodies or other thematic material, having acquired augmented meaning in this way, appear again, or are quoted from, away from their point of origin in order to elicit their corresponding meanings in other contexts. As the name implies, any auxiliary appearances of a theme tend to occur *after* its establishing appearance, typically some emotionally-charged moment earlier in the drama.

Caluori, however, employs the practise freely, regarding the 'definitive' appearance as the source, and all auxiliary appearances as upon a thread reaching from that source in *either* direction over the length of the drama—a thread that he calls a *thematic continuum*. According to the continuum theory, that thread is equivalent to a characteristic psychological aspect of a drama, which is therefore implicitly present over the whole. If that aspect were to be transformed in the course of a drama, the properties of music are such that it can reflect that transformation, even assist in its conveyance. Caluori explains that, because of the phenomenon of musico-literary association, "Any conspicuous musical theme introduced into a drama creates a new thread; each continuum dotted with the various appearances of its distinct thematic material, and each appearance adapted, as necessary, to suit the occasion."

Less complicated than it sounds, the implication of such a comment is that, in fact, *every* instance of an identifiable musical component assumes extra-musical psychological meaning, simply by virtue of being presented in the context of a drama. And therefore all "discrete characteristic formations" — not merely prominent melodic themes — qualify as *constituent forms* (that is, constituent to their respective continua), and might be selected for use elsewhere in a score. In effect, this not only brings the compositional procedures of symphonic development into the theatre, but does so in a way that endows them with complete dramaturgic functionality.

There is a lot of music in *Dangerous Liaisons*, most of it represented more than once. Prominent melodies are constituent forms, but so too are more subtle lines. They can be harmonic or rhythmic, short motives or long phrases, foreground or background, or have any number of other characteristic features. A thorough analysis of the score is beyond the scope of our purpose here, but a quick example makes things plain. Here are two familiar *ostinato* figurations from the *Liaisons* score:

Being characteristic and recognisable, they are susceptible to dramatic association. As such, their appearance constitutes an addition of two new thematic continua to the drama's collection: one new thread for each constituent form; each might be used again and developed, anywhere else in the score—or not. Any additional use of ostinato 1, say, then becomes an instance of that formation's presence along its established continuum.

As it happens, both appear multiple times. Their meanings are not literal and precise, but each does carry its particular psychological colouration, derived from its own inherent construction plus its assimilated dramatic associations: Both are ostinati in relentless [eighth notes]; both outline a tonic minor ninth chord; both are associated with the cunning of the Marquise. Moreover, these examples being accompanimental in quality, their telling presence is easily attached to melody. Ex. 2, for instance, at its source, accompanies the title theme of *"If He Were Here"*, but it opens *"Rumors"* and the *Finale Ultimo* (the *Final Scene*) as accompaniment to one of the letter-writing themes. That one ostinato is in duple meter (4/4), the other triple (3/4), is a calculated option typical of Caluori, encouraging flexible application. One or the other might be included practically anywhere.

An especially remarkable example of thematic reminiscence, which also demonstrates a backwards-reaching instance of thematic continuum, is the case of *"When Silence Reigns"*, the last number in the score. Clearly an important and profound statement, worthy of a theme given commensurate weight. Just as clearly, it can't return again later, after the duet is sung. It is instead teased out here and there as the score proceeds, so as when that final duet arrives, it comes with a sense of familiarity and inevitability. Always appearing in connection with Valmont and Tourvel, it can be spotted during their tense exchange in *"Confrontations"*, and it hovers in a more developed form over the whole of the *Interlude "Tourvel's Despair"* and Valmont's incredible and moving *"Soliloquy"*. Having only appeared during moments of heightened tension, its final, serene return in its definitive, yet not overstated form as the *liebestod* (love-death) brings with it a feeling of resolution, a mysterious breath of transfiguration, fulfilment even, to the otherwise tragic finish.

Incidentally, what *does* appear after the duet, the last few bars of the number that bring the score to its close, is a return of the music from *"She Closes Her Eyes"*, now taking on *its* final meaning. This music, already recalled only moments earlier (as Valmont sends the dying Tourvel his own final message), is a fateful bond between the two lovers. This is no opportunistic turn to flash the theme's inspired melodic *polyphony* at the audience one last time. No, here the theme appears without the voices. Indeed, the melody lines are missing entirely; only the bare accompaniment is played by the orchestra as the curtain comes down, leaving a spellbound hush that one resists breaking despite a vigorous urge to applaud. Along with Steppe's marvellous text, it is because of Caluori's unconventional application of thematic reminiscence that *"When Silence Reigns"* obtains its magical quality.

from Chapter Two: Music and Verse (Phase I)
Fortnight
The next substantial cycle of the collaboration was highlighted by a two-week visit Caluori had managed to arrange, following Steppe's accumulation of several sets of newly written text, including verse for the important numbers, the love duet, *"A Heart To Run To"*, and the unexpected surprise announcement, the Act I *Finale*, a number Steppe called *"Secrets"* — in its entirety. A surprise, because it was a major number which the two had not yet really worked out together (though they had determined the presence of the chorus, and the setting); and because it was presumed by Caluori to be a large scene of a sort that might be tackled later, being more a comment on plot than a part of it.

They had already compared the variations between several of the available versions of the story, and Steppe was especially interested in their differences, in departures from the source, individual solutions and new ideas. He assumed a certain care for originality and had grown keen to distinguish his writing with unique *new* material. His Tourvel's connection with nature, for instance, led to her special affinity for the surrounding park, and to *"The Garden Song"*, a sort of lullaby she turns to for calm. Furthermore, having previously agreed that their treatment of the Volanges character would be as a more comic role, the childless Steppe — whose own mother had no daughters — astoundingly produced the panting and befuddled *"Motherhood"* earlier at the age of nineteen. Solving the ill-defined finale was naturally a foremost consideration for Steppe. *"Secrets"* was an exciting and welcomed new addition; and the score's subsequent reliance upon its important main theme, complementary to that of *the game,* was made possible only by the number's early investiture.

The dedicated collaborative proximity during this rare two-week stint resulted in a remarkable degree of productivity. Pen in hand, Malcolm's tendency to remain poised over his manuscripts, even as he nodded off for thirty minutes here, twenty minutes there, left the impression on the rest of the Steppe household that the composer never slept. In truth, setting the new text to music was not the only work being done during his stay. This time saw the creation of sketches for the instrumentals, "*The Garden*" *Interlude*, and the *Entr'acte* (later becoming the *Prelude* to the *Intermedio*, prior to Act II), and new numbers were also being written whilst the two were together. His visit being finite, the multitude of ideas and details afforded by the days of extended mutual attentiveness to various dramatic solutions simply wouldn't wait for a full night of "lying dormant in a bed."

The music for "*A Heart To Run To*" was amongst the first tasks to which Caluori set himself, understanding that the obligatory popular love duet for Tourvel and Valmont would provide musical material central to the story of the two characters. But it was precisely this almost formulaic, cliché expectation of a popular style for the duet that Caluori found so distasteful. "So be it," he now says, with a good-humoured shrug. "But there was no *way* a drum beat was going in there." In cooperation with Steppe's verse, however, the music does achieve the delicate accomplishment of buoying the lovers' fragile, uncertain union to a heady place of impulsive mutual surrender, intimating even from Valmont a sense of genuine sincerity.

It's in the auxiliary treatment of the duet's music that Caluori later reclaims some of the sophistication that was sacrificed at its source. In view of its thematic continuum, music from "*A Heart To Run To*" is first introduced in the number "*Madame de Tourvel*", the scene that also first introduces her character in the original version of the score. Here Caluori applies a fairly extended representation of the theme — its arrival accentuated by a brightening modulation of key — to Tourvel's words as she reflects upon the surrounding nature.

Something in a garden
Is very close to God.
Quiet, still, and innocent,
Beauty so unflawed.

> *Simple in its splendor,*
> *Modest in its grace,*
> *It's so easy to surrender*
> *To this quiet, perfect place.*

The theme later appears, fully and at ease, as *"The Garden" Interlude*, when Tourvel escapes to the out of doors from the discomfort of the awkward fuss Valmont had created about her inside. And still again, as the dread-filled *Interlude "Tourvel's Departure"*, she here withdrawing from the manor altogether. Such striking usages as these, preceding—as they do—the arrival of the *definitive* presentation, *"A Heart To Run To"*, convey the theme as being, in fact, related specifically to Tourvel. More particularly, its associations are with the feelings of safety and rightness, the sense of home and simple peace that she finds in nature and ascribes to the Divine.

Conversely then, when used in Valmont's music, the theme initially flashes past, flaring up only to then quickly dissipate, in his attempts to capture Tourvel's guarded trust. In his progress, successive quotations of the theme do increasingly endure. But only upon the arrival of the duet, in full bloom, does he prevail in unlocking the path to Tourvel's deep inner place of comfort and security. The unbound approach to the placement of themes within a continuum—not limited to a post-duet reminiscence—is what thus enables the dramaturgic aspect of the music to assume such complex semantic revelations as these.

Between composer and librettist, there was always the presumption, music-first or text-first, that the list of unwritten numbers contained items for each collaborator, and that their respective work would proceed concurrently. Neither wanted to be idle. The approach seemed sensible enough, especially with the songs-first guideline in place. And, for the time being, the presumption survived. Although there were practical limitations to when music might be written first, Caluori wouldn't wait for a section of libretto to be provided in advance, if his inspiration was matched with a permissive circumstance.

When Cécile, for example, upset by her night time encounter with Valmont, rushes to the Marquise for advice in *"Cécile's Confession"*, the scene's opening had already been determined: Cécile suddenly bursts onto the scene, anxiously spouting her confidences to the Marquise, who then advises her, coolly and persuasively, leading Cécile astray to satisfy her own ends. Needing only this scenario as inspiration, Caluori was able to write an appropriately agitated entrance for Cécile, directly followed by a fervent theme originally referred to as the 'pity' motive ("Madame, it was Valmont...."), though, regarding its continuum, it is more properly understood as a statement of impassioned discontent. The Marquise's reply uses the music of her *Vow*, adapting it to become "more seductive." This music was, in turn, enough inspiration for Steppe to then create a first draft of the balance of the ensuing exchange between the two characters, basing his verse, fittingly, on music from *"The Game"* and from *"The Seduction"*.

* * *

Following the composer's departure, the residual momentum of the fortnight assisted Steppe in his preparations of three key supporting scenes, including the *"Mail"* scene, depicting Valmont's first movements against Tourvel. He knows that she's already been receiving letters of warning from someone. When the sordid interception of her letters was later consolidated into this scene, Caluori added a sort of incidental coda to his original setting, following Tourvel's flight from the room. The underscore is a mellifluous, winding and pacing melody line, a brooding belligerence, as Valmont reads from a misplaced letter. And with the building musical tension that overtakes the scene's conclusion with heaving infuriation as he reaches the name of the signatory, Caluori knew at once that this music would be heard again—as the blistering standoff that makes confidants into adversaries, in *"The Argument"*.

Also penned at this time was Steppe's enchanting duet, *"If Only"*, his delightful depiction of youth's hesitant fascination with love. Cécile and Dançeny, finally alone together after great pains taken on their behalf to—shall we say—hearten their coupling, never get round to singing any of the love duet's lines to each other, each longing for an encouraging sign from the other. In two of the later, reminiscent uses of the number's refrain, Steppe eloquently transmutes the hopeful, yearning thought of 'if only...' into a lament for things which needn't have come to pass: serving first to introduce Cécile's *Reprise "The Game"*, then poignantly invoked in the *Finale Ultimo*, between Danceny and Valmont, upon their impending duel.

Knowing Caluori's intent to sew his themes throughout, as the writing turned from 'songs' to 'scenes', Steppe determined musical content with increased measure, supplying verse interlaced here and there with instances of existing music. In a revision to *"The Key"*, Steppe inserted music from *"If Only"* as a phrase for Cécile. Its occurrence, as she puts her unwanted doubts to Valmont, is a very fine touch ("Monsieur, do you think that is wise?"...). Still learning about life beyond convent walls, Cécile sees Valmont as a gentleman and a friend. Now, he's tempting the girl to steal for him the key to her bedroom with an offer to secretly pass Danceny's letters to her. Not only does Steppe's prosody beautifully match Cécile's words to the inflection of the musical line, but as the phrase caries her to an all-too-easy acquiescence, the librettist's very choice of theme marks the moment with an adept stroke of musical dramatisation, speaking beyond his own libretto. Through *"If Only"*, Cécile's longing for Danceny overrides her rational concerns. *Any* reply from Valmont is adequate reassurance; she's already convinced herself. Not, in fact, gullibly persuaded of Valmont's plan as the right thing to do, Cécile is *choosing*—independent of his dishonesty—to cross a line.

Thirdly, Rosemonde's *"The Nature of Man"* instructs that a woman's natural inclination to give love, if indulged with a man, leads to inescapable despair. Those familiar with the classic story might here anticipate a guarded sermon of lonely cynicism, born of life's hard lessons, as argued to one's audience in the manner of a Tim Rice. But the extreme attitude of Rosemonde's stark words, in Steppe's hands, that men are lusty warriors, traitorous schemers, unreasonably selfish, entirely fickle and yet unforgiving, is mere groundwork. Recall that the 'seasons' of Tourvel are those of innocent purity, of life's goodness, and God's love. Steppe once again summons the idea of seasons, as Tourvel's mentor here imparts three other senses of the metaphor, to underscore the lesson. *The passage of time:* in all her years, things have always been this way; *the certainty of the cycle:* the path she warns of progresses to one destination only; *the force of nature:* it is the unalterable way of the world.

If there is a message for the audience, Steppe's noted interest in the story's "stratification of gender" magnifies it to make the point. In such a world, where men entertain their free and reckless reign, the distorted inequality of the sexes has left only monsters or misery. Tourvel's mentor, Rosemonde, espouses the imperilled resign of the marginalized woman; whereas Cécile's mentor, the Marquise, an uncompromising, ruthless determination to share equally in the spoils of men's wars—nay, but to indeed outdo them.

A rare extant worksheet illustrates the progressive stages of Caluori's procedure for setting Steppe's text to *"The Nature of Man"*—a more operatically conceived number, one of the few that he actually calls *aria* in the score. On the worksheet, after first breaking down the schematic of Steppe's stanzas and identifying three phrase types (A1, A2, and B), Caluori begins with a 'rhythm sketch', exploring and determining patterns that work with the language used in all instances of each given phrase type. Functional rhythms having been established, they are then converted into melody. The page reveals a gradual evolution of multiple time signatures, melodic possibilities, and key areas, into the composer's eventually accepted form.

Caluori's working copy of the libretto is, as well, scrawled throughout with annotations indicating how the music should be constructed. Margin notes identify stanzas assigned with any particular musical themes. Jottings might detail pacing and transitions, remark on structure, or indicate special connections to observe. One occasionally finds verse with barlines drawn between words, short underscores specifying syllabic stress and downbeats, or lines of text with their poetic *scansion* fully marked. Indicators of a form of shorthand rhythm sketch, likely leading to a process similar to that described above, in the composer's study of potential musical settings.

A penchant for organised relationships, and a spirit of exploration and solution are a composer's calling cards. The writing of *Dangerous Liaisons* was by this point well underway, and the collaborators felt as though they were beginning to settle into a familiar routine. Quietly in the background, however, as a matter of course, Caluori's instincts were constantly observing the ways in which the two collaborative contributions bear on one another, text first or music first. Songs versus scenes, declamation versus narrative versus dialogue versus recitative — pros and cons, the quality of the creative result, and a persistence for uncovering the 'best' way. The ordinary proceedings of Caluori's subsequent *routine* would involve an unperceived chain of cumulative events, spurring an unparalleled reorientation of the collaboration itself, ultimately leading to a point of illumination that, in retrospect, might be argued to have been on the cards since the composer first engaged the project.

Melpomene hopes you enjoyed these samples from *Killing Valmont*, by D. Hector Francis. For more information visit:
www.KillingValmont.com

"... Mr. Francis' bold yet reader-friendly look into the dynamic relationships between music, libretto, and underlying drama ... [considers] the stuff that really makes musical drama tick. I think even I have learned a few things about Dangerous Liaisons."

Malcolm Caluori

CREATING THE MUSIC

By Malcolm Caluori

LES LIAISONS DANGEREUSES is a classic French novel from which several film versions and stage plays have sprung, even opera and musical theatre. Its melodramatic nature is very operatic, and cries out to be set to music. But the nature of the story, the characters, and the complexities of the plot demand the grittier performance, faster pace and flexibilities that are afforded in a musical, that you just can't pull off as well in pure opera. It's a provocative psychological tragedy examining virtue in a society of vice, the frictions of imbalance around such issues as stature and gender, and the importance of recognizing the genuine humanity within one's self versus "putting it on" for one's own gain. Ours, though classically flavored, is a large-scale, Broadway-type show that draws from the features of both worlds, falling somewhere in between musical theatre and opera.

This is a period story, and when Johnathan and I took on the project we decided *almost* immediately to keep it in its original setting. This decision led me to make several choices about how I wanted the music to sound, and the show itself to feel. With any period in history comes a period in musical history. With this show, at least as far as the setting is concerned, we are dealing with the specific musical atmosphere of the French Baroque, bringing with it a rich milieu of developing musical forms, the birth of chamber music and, handily enough, a strong social and artistic focus on the phenomenal rise of opera.

This *Dangerous Liaisons* is not a period piece; it is not a Baroque opera. But, absent television and radio, there was a strong convergence of music with the life of the eighteenth century aristocrat, needful of entertainment. I felt that it was not only necessary, but also inevitable that the taste of the score should involve more than mere indications of the music of the period. It was important to embroider the sounds of the time into the score in order to take the audience into the world of these characters.

So in the (unapologetically tonal) score one can expect the drama of each scene to be told using musical devices of our own time, but tinged with, say, rhythms characteristic to the period, and the sounds of a harpsichord, or perhaps a pair of recorders. Further, there are no low brass instruments in the orchestration, only horns and a single trumpet. The style is lyric drama. A number of orchestral interludes and the heavy use of *arioso* and *parlante* further blurs the lines between opera and musical theatre, and a strong nod to Baroque *recitative* helps to lend a sense of period. You'll find, also, parody of the comic *opera buffa*, and the occasional spoken line glancing toward French *opéra comique*. The score includes instances of rondeau, minuet, and chamber music in the style of the French Baroque; and I especially enjoyed writing the polyphony of the several vocal ensembles, also derived from operatic technique.

Perhaps the boldest statement made with regard to this sensibility is to be found in the Intermedio. An entire structural element unto itself, it presents the back-story of the Marquise. Independent of the ongoing plot, this important background is presented between the two acts, in the form of a variety of vignettes involving situation drama and dance, reminiscent of the intermezzi that were performed between the acts of operas in the Baroque period, though musically it is very different. As the Italian term *intermezzo* evolved in meaning to later include purely instrumental works, I deliberately chose the older term *intermedio*, in order to specifically invoke the original practice of the mini-drama given between acts.

But even considering such stylistic references, the score also features lullaby, patter song, two big waltz numbers, Latin chant, liebestod, a mad scene, even barbershop quartet. As composer, still the drama itself must always come first. Any special elements employed should be selected and used in the service of telling the story. And this story, in particular, is so dense that there really is no room for empty indulgence. Everything packed into the score must be functional, efficient, and revealing, *as well* as imaginative and entertaining. Caught in a reality where one either misleads or is misled, the characters presented in Johnathan's libretto are deeply human, each navigating insecurity in a unique way. The many-layered quality of this timeless story — dynamic layers of character, atmosphere, facade and psychology — well befits today's eclectic artistic expression. Our workboxes are now stocked with such variety, of style, of color, of technique; the game of choosing for the dramatic need at hand has made this score a joy to create.

Dangerous Liaisons
Complete Original Concept

A Musical Dramatization
by Malcolm Caluori and Johnathan Daniel Steppe
based on the novel *Les Liaisons Dangereuses*
by Pierre Choderlos de Laclos

Music
Malcolm Caluori

Libretto
Johnathan Daniel Steppe

Characters and Original Recorded Cast

The Marquise de Merteuil (Mezzo-Soprano)
Maura Carey Neill

The Vicomte de Valmont (Baritone)
Shaun Whitley

Madame de Tourvel (Soprano)
Rachael Henderson

Cécile Volanges (Soprano)
Kristie Krabe

Madame de Volanges (Mezzo-Soprano)
Christy Brumfield Baggett

Madame de Rosemonde (Contralto)
Ginger Rosen

The Chevalier Dançeny (Tenor)
John Young

From the chorus: Gossips (trio), Hunters (quartet), Socialites (sextet), Young Girls (trio); and several comprimario and incidental roles.

The chorus ensemble serves throughout as:
Opera Chorus/Patrons, Party Guests, Gala Crowd, Nuns, Spectators

Maura Carey Neill (Marquise)

Shaun Whitley (Valmont)

Rachael Henderson (Tourvel)

Kristie Krabe (Cécile)

Christy Baggett (Volanges)

John Young (Dançeny)

Ginger Rosen (Rosemonde)   Tad Wilson (Commandeur)

Synopsis

Prologue: "The Vow"
In the last days of Pre-Revolutionary France, the aristocracy gather for entertainment and scandal. Among them, the Vicomte de Valmont, and the Marquise de Merteuil, once lovers and still long-time partners in secret games of seduction. The marquise learns that a former lover who abandoned her for another has become engaged to Cécile Volanges, the virginal daughter of her cousin, Madame de Volanges. Recognizing the girl as her opportunity, the marquise vows vengeance, and determines to enlist her confidante, the notorious Valmont, to take the young girl before her marriage.

Act I–Part 1
Valmont refuses to assist the marquise in this matter, confessing that he has already met his next conquest, the pious and happily married Madame de Tourvel, at the country estate of his aunt, Madame de Rosemonde, where she is a guest. But his advances toward the marquise inspire her to strike a deal: one night of passion together as reward for his victory over Tourvel.

Turning her attentions to Cécile, the marquise orchestrates a secret meeting between Cécile and the Chevalier Dançeny, a poor young music teacher who Madame de Volanges hires to instruct her daughter. Although Cécile and Dançeny do fall in love, as the marquise hoped, the chevalier remains respectful of Cécile, and Cécile remains a virgin. Meanwhile at the Rosemonde estate, Valmont succeeds, through a series of staged encounters, in gaining Madame de Tourvel's friendship. Knowing his reputation, Tourvel sees Valmont as a soul to be saved. Yet the connection between them slowly grows deeper. Still, Valmont overplays his hand when he confesses his love to her, and she asks that he leave the estate. Obliged by his own words, Valmont leaves the country.

Act I–Part 2

Upon his return to Paris, Valmont agrees to take Cécile himself, as revenge on her mother whom he had discovered was warning Tourvel against him. The marquise devises a plan in which Valmont can pursue both Cécile and Tourvel at the same time. She betrays Cécile's correspondence with Dançeny to the girl's mother, Volanges, advising her to accept an invitation to the Château Rosemonde, thus separating Cécile from Dançeny. Volanges agrees, and the marquise promises to join them shortly thereafter. Separately, she encourages Cécile to continue her liaison in secret. Now headed back to his aunt's château, Valmont consoles Dançeny, promising to deliver his letters to Cécile.

Valmont's return to Rosemonde's interrupts a supper party and, as tensions mount, Valmont succeeds in upsetting Tourvel, who retreats to the garden for fresh air. He follows and, though at first she spurns his presence, her growing feelings lead them to an uneasy reconciliation. She later begins to recognize her growing vulnerability, as does Valmont, who confidently reassures the marquise of his steady progress.

Fulfilling his other promise, Valmont sneaks into Cécile's room where he forces himself on her. Using blackmail and the girl's own ignorance, he succeeds in his dark seduction. Elsewhere, ignorant, Dançeny optimistically holds on to the hope that he and Cécile might yet have a future together. Distressed, Cécile turns to the recently arrived marquise for help, who corrupts her with advise to continue learning the art of lovemaking from Valmont, to free herself from her mother by agreeing to the marriage, and to keep Dançeny as a secret lover.

A gala ball is given at the Rosemonde estate, where Tourvel finds herself on the brink of forbidden love, Cécile wonders at the startling changes her life has taken, and Valmont sees himself poised for victory. Ever the secret manipulator, the marquise watches from afar, all of her pawns in place and checkmate only a few moves away.

INTERMEDIO: "REFLECTIONS"
In a letter written to Valmont, the marquise recounts a sequence of experiences from her past. She explains the evolution of her personal philosophy, attempting to rationally justify her uncompromising, wicked nature.

ACT II
Valmont Continues his sexual education of Cécile, and his pursuit of Tourvel, who finally relents to her growing attraction. Moved by compassion, however, Valmont hesitates and Tourvel flees the château at Rosemonde's insistence. Furious at his weakness, Valmont pursues Tourvel to Paris, where he and Tourvel at last give in to their passion.

As the marquise entertains her maid with storytelling, they are interrupted by Valmont, who attempts to claim his prize from the marquise. She rejects his demand and cancels their bargain, claiming that he is now in love with Tourvel. Later, as Volanges worries about her daughter's behavior, Valmont cites his successful ruining of Cécile, who has now secretly miscarried, as further reason why the marquise should acquiesce. But the marquise is adamant: Valmont must leave Tourvel and betray her love.

Tourvel has indeed fallen in love with Valmont, and has broken from her husband. But when she joyously greets Valmont, he cruelly rejects her, fulfilling the marquise's wishes. As Valmont rushes to the marquise, Tourvel collapses from anguish. Still, the love that has grown between Valmont and Tourvel creates a further rift between the two former lovers, and one-time allies begin a steady march toward enmity. Valmont discovers Dançeny in the marquise's bed and, after sending the boy away, gives the marquise an ultimatum, which she fiercely rejects.

Moved by pride and now bent on revenge, Valmont and the marquise turn their treachery upon each other. As the climax approaches, secrets are revealed and passions explode with unexpected and deadly consequences. The resulting endgame can have no victor, as the true price of this most dangerous game is at last revealed.

Libretto

Dangerous Liaisons
COMPLETE ORIGINAL CONCEPT

By Johnathan Daniel Steppe

A vertical mark indicates lines that are heard simultaneously.

CAUTION: Professionals and amateurs are hereby warned that this material, being fully protected under the Copyright Laws of the United States of America and all other countries of the Berne and Universal Copyright Conventions, is subject to a royalty. All rights including, but not limited to, professional and amateur stage performing, recording, motion picture, recitation, lecturing, public reading, radio and television broadcasting, and the rights of translation into foreign languages are expressly reserved. Particular emphasis is placed on the question of readings and all uses of this book by educational institutions, permission for which must be secured from the copyright holder.

CD1

Prologue: "The Vow"

1.1

The Grand Foyer of the Commedie Italienne, in Paris. At rise, the stage is dim. A Baroque string orchestra begins to play. The clear sound of a tenor is heard.

TENOR:
Andiamo udire il mare,
Sussurare con la dea di dare.
Non ha mancanza di sogni e serenità.
Che giorni gioiosi di vitalità!
Ci abbiamo e pace e felicità!

(The chorus takes up the tune and, gradually, the Grand Foyer is revealed. The hall is empty at present, and the sounds of the chorus come from beyond a set of double doors that leads into the theatre.)

CHORUS:
Andiamo udire il mare,
etc.

1.2

(A bit of dance music signals the conclusion of the piece. Personnel in theater livery begin to appear, straightening their wigs, tightening their gloves, etc. They take up positions beside the doors leading to the inner theater. Applause is heard from within. Finally, the doors open with a flourish, spilling the aristocratic patrons in to fill the hall. A man and woman meet down stage. They whisper to each other, she hiding her words from the rest of the crowd with her fan.)

MAN 1:
What a stunning evening!

WOMAN 1:
Everyone's performing!

YOUNG COUPLE:
(Approaching the edge of the stage)
If you just look around you...

ALL PATRONS:
Here's to opera, prima donnas,
Long cadenzas, short refrains,
Whispers in secluded boxes,
Fans that hide a kiss
You don't want explained.

GIDDY WOMAN:
Powdered coifs are now the trend.

YOUNG PRUDE:
Poor maréchale was born to spend...

MAN 1:
(Pointing)
They were once the best of friends.

YOUNG PRUDE:
...Far beyond her dividends.

MAN 2:
If he loves her, why pretend?

DANÇENY:
Did you see the opera's end?

PATRONS:
Damn the opera! Here's to scandal,
Bourgeoisie-esque rendezvous!
Who needs opera? Who needs Handel?
Give us secrets, give us news!

(The patrons break down into small groups of gossipers. A woman moves excitedly to a group at the front of the stage.)

WOMAN 1:
Did you hear who just arrived,
Looking fresh and quite revived,
From a tryst with the sisters Dumont?

WOMAN 2:
(Interrupting)
Valmont!

MAN 1:
Valmont?

WOMAN 1:
(Taking over again)
That Don Juan of a debutante!

MAN 2:
Valmont!

WOMAN 2:
Valmont!
The vicomte with the name to flaunt.

(The gossip passes to another group.)

GIDDY WOMAN:
Did you hear Valmont is here?

OLD WOMAN:
(To her deaf old husband)
The Vicomte de Valmont, dear.

GIDDY WOMAN:
He's the man all Paris fears.

EFFEMINATE MAN:
Quite the love-bent buccaneer.

TWO MEN:
Hide your daughters, hide your wives!

DEAF OLD MAN:
If you don't, they won't survive.

WOMAN 1:
It's the vicomte!

TWO MEN:
Not the vicomte!

WOMAN 2:
Yes, the vicomte!

EFFEMINATE MAN:
Here's the vicomte!

PATRONS:
Make way for the Vicomte de Valmont!

(M. le Vicomte de Valmont enters as the patrons part. They form an informal line down which he makes his way, kissing a hand here and there, nodding at several of the men. There is a great range of emotions regarding him, from pure lust, to grudging admiration, to controlled loathing. Toward the end of the line, finally, M. de LeCroix speaks.)

LECROIX: Is that him, the great seducer and terror of all Paris? You must be joking!

(He laughs scornfully. Valmont approaches him amiably.)

VALMONT:
Monsieur de LeCroix,
Bonjour, good evening.
How's your wife?
Did she ever recover
From the time she was my lover?

LECROIX:
You bastard, I'll kill you!
You'll pay with your life!

(LeCroix lunges for Valmont, but his friends restrain him. Valmont gives them a mock bow then continues on, looking for someone.)

PATRONS (WOMEN):
The Vicomte de Valmont is on the prowl,
But who is he here to see?
Let's hope the poor woman who runs afoul
Of the vicomte tonight
has made her peace with God.

Only one woman has dared resist him.
Only one woman can hold her own.
Only one woman can dare to list him
Among her friends, one woman alone.

(Valmont has made his way up center, where a gathered group parts respectfully, revealing Mme. la Marquise de Merteuil, who sits fanning herself. Valmont kneels before her, and she offers a hand to kiss.)

MARQUISE:
Valmont!

WOMAN 3: The Marquise de Merteuil!

MARQUISE:
I think you've come a bit too late.
The curtain was at eight.
Were you otherwise engaged?
I should be enraged at this neglect.
Show some respect, my friend.

VALMONT:
I didn't mean to make you wait,
And I'm set to demonstrate
That I'm nothing without you.

MARQUISE:
Vicomte, that will do.

As charming as ever, I see, and as dangerous. If I were another woman, I would fear for my reputation, talking here with you.

VALMONT: And if I were any other man, I would fear for mine.

MARQUISE: Hold you tongue, vicomte! My reputation is questioned by no one. All of Paris knows that.

VALMONT: And only I know better.

MARQUISE: How fortunate then, that we are not two other people.

You, you and I,
We know each other well.
So tell me,
What device detained you?

VALMONT: I've spent the day packing, actually.

MARQUISE: Packing? You're leaving Paris? Whatever for? Ah, don't tell me. You've finally found another maiden who has yet to be robbed of her virginity?

VALMONT: You wound me! I'm going to visit my aunt in the country.

MARQUISE: *(Amused)*
Your aunt, Madame de Rosemonde?

> Valmont, you must be out of your mind.
> The country life just isn't your kind.
> Unless I am mistaken,
> I sense something of a plan.
> A story you must now expand.
> Can you tell me?
> Valmont, you're a horrible man.

VALMONT:
> Yes, you are right,
> There is more than I say,
> A reason enough for my leaving.
> But now's not the time
> And this isn't the place
> To speak of my greatest of plans.

MARQUISE:
> Your greatest of plans?
> What?
> Seducing some poor country girl?

VALMONT: All in good time, ma chére. Please forgive this sudden departure, and trust me to explain everything when I write you.

MARQUISE: And write you must, soon. You know how I love to receive your letters.

VALMONT: Almost as much as you love to receive me?

MARQUISE:
  You, you and I...
  That was so long ago,
  Like water passing beneath
  The highest bridge.
  I must be off.

VALMONT:
  Where are you going?

MARQUISE: My cousin, Madame de Volanges, is having a party for her daughter. A homecoming of sorts. The girl is returning from the convent, where she has been receiving a Christian education.

VALMONT: Her daughter, Cécile?

MARQUISE: The very same.

VALMONT: A lovely creature.

MARQUISE: And unknown to her, already engaged, the poor fool. The happiest day of my life, vicomte, was when my husband graciously died and left me his fortune. I am curious to find out the identity of the auspicious groom, however. And the identity of the woman who's taking you from me.

  Who is she, vicomte?

VALMONT: What?

MARQUISE:
  You don't have to say.
  I know you too well, and you'll tell me.
  In time I know all that you do.

VALMONT:
  That is true.
  Farewell, now, my greatest of friends.

MARQUISE:
  Adieu, vicomte.
  Good luck on your way.
  Whenever you write,
  Leave nothing unsaid.

(MARQUISE)
Now I'm off to see Madame de Volanges.

1.3

(The scene shifts to the salon of Madame de Volanges. The patrons at the opera become the guests at Volanges' party. They freeze in tableau, glasses raised to toast Mme. de Volanges, who is poised to address the crowd.)

GUESTS:
(Breaking their freeze)
Here's to marriage, pros'prous unions,
Bridal beds and wedding vows!
Bless the mother and her daughter,
Bless her innocence, for now anyhow!

VOLANGES:
Thank you all for coming.
My this evening's been so splendid.
But my daughter doesn't know
Of her engagement;
There are details to be made...
Hush! Here she comes!

(Cécile Volanges and her maid enter. Madame de Volanges barely avoids a passing servant, her wine glass coming perilously close to tipping. A gentleman guest steadies her; she smiles at him as Cécile takes her place at her mother's side.)

GENTLEMAN GUEST:
Madame de Volanges,
Here's to you and your charming daughter
On this happy night
When she returns from convent life.

I hope she'll find Paris to her liking,
And one day soon
Make a lucky man his wife!

VOLANGES:
Hush, monsieur, hush!
Mingle everyone!

(Volanges' major domo enters with the marquise.)

GUESTS:
Pour the wine and let's be merry!
Let's not speak a 'marry' word.
Winks and whispers, sighs and smiles,
Life is now for the absurd!

MAJOR DOMO: Presenting the Marquise de Merteuil!

VOLANGES:
(Rushing to the marquise)
Cousin!
I'd been convinced you wouldn't show.
But now we're comme-il-faut!

MARQUISE:
I was otherwise engaged.
Please, don't be enraged.
It was Valmont who detained me.

VOLANGES:
Valmont?
The devil himself!
Did he come as well?

MARQUISE: No, no.

VOLANGES: Thank the Lord!
The women he has ruined now are countless.

MARQUISE: Not to worry. He's off to the country to visit his old aunt, Mme. de Rosemonde. Paris can breathe easily for a while.

VOLANGES: That's a blessing, anyhow.

MARQUISE:
But now where is Cécile?
The dear girl must be exhausted.

VOLANGES:
Over there.
Look at her standing there.
My baby, my future, my prize.

MARQUISE:
And the husband?
Where's the groom-to-be?

1.4

(She begins to lead the marquise to M. le Comte de Gercourt)

VOLANGES:
On this I must ask you to keep a secret.
I've yet to announce him, but you I can tell.
I want you to meet him, he's right over here.
Marquise de Merteuil, meet the Comte de Gercourt.

(Gercourt turns with a smile, which freezes as he sees the marquise. She, in turn, regards him coldly.)

MARQUISE:
Monsieur de Gercourt,
We've already met.

GERCOURT:
Ah yes, we have.
Quite a long time ago.

MARQUISE:
Not quite long enough.

VOLANGES: Oh my Lord... Did you say Valmont was going to the Rosemonde estate?

MARQUISE: Yes, what's the matter?

VOLANGES: I just remembered. A dear friend of mine, Madame de Tourvel, is visiting there. Her husband is away on business and... Oh, God! She'll be defenseless... I must write her immediately! Please, excuse me!

(She rushes offstage to find a servant)

MARQUISE: Madame de Tourvel?

GERCOURT: You know her?

MARQUISE: Not well.

Not as well as I once knew you.

Once before we shared many pleasures,
Before you found another to please.
No one's ever scorned me as you did.
You should get down on your knees...

GERCOURT:
Let's not start this.

It's over.
We've been through all of this before.
We had a fling and nothing more.

MARQUISE:
You are still such a bore.

GERCOURT:
Why waste my breath to argue?
What's left to say?

MARQUISE:
You used me, Gercourt!

GERCOURT:
For love is sometimes fleeting.
Madame, adieu.

(He leaves her. She watches him retreat into the crowd.)

MARQUISE:
How the tangle of sheets
Can give way to feelings of hate!
When, in boredom, a lover retreats,
Passion turns upon itself.

It isn't as if I ever loved you.
It's not about love, but pride.
It's I who must say an affair is over.
It's I who says when passion's died.

(Turning her attention to Cécile, who stands nearby sipping a drink.)
At last I'll see you pay, you'll play the fool for everyone.
Your bride-to-be will be the key to seeing you undone.
I swear this now, I take this vow to turn her path to sin!
For what I want I'll need Valmont, so let the game begin!

(The marquise exits, determined.)

Act I–Part 1

1.5
Prelude

Throughout the transitionary prelude, the Volanges supper party ebbs and finally disperses. Volanges, kissing Cécile goodnight, exits, leaving Cécile alone, as the stage focus shifts to Cécile's boudoir.

1.6
Correspondences 1

Cécile in her boudoir. She collapses at her writing desk, takes a moment to enjoy her fatigue, then takes out a sheet of paper, dips quill into ink, and begins to write.

CÉCILE:
My Sophie, dearest friend,
I'm at last in Paris.
Life here is so amazing,
As you said it'd be.

I have my own maid now,
And my own room,
A harp and a desk
With a lock and key.

(Standing, continuing, she gradually moves toward an area of the stage now established as Madame de Volanges' salon.)

Now Sophie, here's the news:
I think I'm to be wed!
That's what my maid has whispered—
She's an awful tease.

Yesterday a young man
Came to see me.
Maman called me down.
Could this man be he?

(Arriving in the salon, a shoemaker and Volanges wait for her.)

I must be brave,
Must act with grace.
This man had come to be my husband!

SHOEMAKER:
Ah, mademoiselle!

VOLANGES:
My daughter, sir.

SHOEMAKER:
A charming girl, you do me honor.

Let's not be shy.
Please have a seat.
I'm truly eager to begin.

CÉCILE:
(Sitting by the shoemaker who takes hold of her foot.)
Sophie, I was never sicker.
What would he begin?
All around me the air grew thicker.

SHOEMAKER:
(Removing one of her shoes.)
If we're to find
The perfect size...

CÉCILE:
He drew closer...
Grabbed my ankle!
Would undress me so it seemed!

(The shoemaker turns to Volanges and holds up a shoe, which Volanges finds to her liking. Cécile cannot see what is transpiring.)

SHOEMAKER / VOLANGES:
How perfect!

CÉCILE:
So, I screamed!

(Cécile lets out a shriek as the shoemaker turns, startling him and thereby causing him to snap the heel off of the shoe. Volanges gives a small laugh. The lights dim on Volanges and the shoemaker, growing brighter on Cécile, who returns to her desk.)

(CÉCILE):
And so,
I frightened off the best shoemaker in Paris.
But how could I know?

Convents teach of sins and scriptures,
Not of sizing shoes.
There're far too many don'ts and dos.
How will I ever learn?

(The lights fade on Cécile, and rise on Volanges, now at her own desk writing a letter, the shoemaker gone. Lights also rise separately on Madame de Tourvel, who reads from Volanges' letter.)

VOLANGES:
Then the shoemaker left
And Cécile started weeping,
Ah well, she is young and will learn.
But now onto my purpose
For writing this letter;
Madame, I've a warning to give.

The Vicomte de Valmont will be coming
To Madame de Rosemonde's where you stay.
He endangers your virtue
And good reputation.
Please come back to Paris today.

(The focus returns to Cécile, now back in her room, and also shifts to the marquise, upstage on a raised platform. She too is writing a letter.)

MARQUISE:
Dear Vicomte,
You must come back to Paris today,
I've a wish and it must be obeyed.
Valmont, don't be difficult,
Vengeance and love will be served
If you come to my aid.

My cousin Cécile is to marry,
And Gercourt has been promised her hand!
You recall when he left me
For your ugly mistress;
We both have a debt to be paid.

(MARQUISE):
    She must be ruined!
    Her virginity has to be taken.
    It is the prize
    That Gercourt values most in a woman.

    Youthful she lies,
    Like a rosebud just waiting to waken.
    Think of Gercourt.
    He'll be played for the fool that he is.

CÉCILE:
    Still no word, not a sign.
    Did I make a mistake?
    Life can be so confusing
    When you're all grown up.

    Maybe they won't tell me
    For my own sake.
    If blindness is bliss,
    I'm the happy fool!

(The light switches to Valmont, who is on a platform adjacent to the marquise's. He responds with a letter of his own.)

VALMONT:
    Dearest Marquise,
    There's no call for my help in this matter.
    What is this girl
    But a fountain of ignorant chatter?

    Any young sap could seduce her,
    Just take a look at her.
    She is so young,
    She knows nothing but how to give in.

(Lights fade on Cécile, and rise on Tourvel in the gardens of the Château Rosemonde.)

(VALMONT):
>   But my newest adventure
>   Is much more appealing,
>   An obstacle sure to enchant.
>   Madame de Tourvel,
>   Who is known for her virtue,
>   Is spending some time with my aunt.
>
>   The sanctity of her religion,
>   A husband she loves more than life —
>   She's a prize to be won,
>   And you know when it comes
>   To refusing a challenge I can't.

(Lights fade on Tourvel.)

MARQUISE:
>   Please, vicomte, are you joking?
>   You must be afflicted.
>   This woman's a horrible bore.
>   If she gives in at all
>   It will still be half-hearted,
>   Her passion runs cold to its core.

VALMONT:
>   Therein lies the challenge I'm seeking,
>   To see her at last unrestrained.

MARQUISE:
>   I don't see the challenge,
>   A husband is nothing.
>   To me, infidelity's plain.

VALMONT:
(Gradually drifting to the marquise's platform)
Must I explain?
I don't want her to give in too quickly.
I want to see
How she struggles in vain to resist me.

Certain she'll fall,
And yet still she proceeds indiscreetly.
Once and for all,
She will find that her God is a joke.

MARQUISE:
Please explain.
How ridiculous then, to proceed.
If you turn back right now, I won't tell.

I think it is best,
Vicomte, I sense danger.
You're speaking so carelessly,
look at yourself!
You've a name to uphold,
Don't become a joke.

(They arrive face to face.)

VALMONT:
Madame, you worry too much.
Have I ever lost when love is the game?

MARQUISE: Of course not. Why else would we be together? I have much respect for you, vicomte. You're the only person who can rival me in both seduction and deceit. Still, the greatest virtuosos often are the one's who are ultimately consumed by their work.

VALMONT: You underestimate me. I promise you, before I'm finished, this woman will sacrifice her every virtue to me, and unable to relieve her torment elsewhere, will find comfort only in my arms. Delicious irony.

1.7
SOMETHING MORE THAN LOVE

MARQUISE: She does enchant you, doesn't she?

VALMONT: It's a passing charm. Once I've conquered her...

MARQUISE: Destroyed her...

VALMONT: Then, I'll move on.

MARQUISE:
That's what I like about you, vicomte,
So cold, so cruel, so sweet.
I knew you were my perfect match.
From the start we were destined to meet.

You, you and I,
We are the perfect pair,
Unlike those lovers who waste their time in love.

You, you and I,
We have a diff'rent affair,
For we have found something more than love.

Something to last
When love goes its way.
Vengeance and power
Together and sweet as the day.

You and I will go on and on.
Our story is never done,
Because we have found something more than love.

VALMONT:
You, you I felt
Before we ever touched.
You held me captive with nothing but a glance.

Now, here we are.
We've shared and seen so much,
And we have found something more than love.

(VALMONT):
> We've made the choice
> To love and be free.
> Nothing can hold us,
> We've moved past the highest degree.

MARQUISE:
> The decision was easy to see.
> It's what we had to be.
> We've moved past the highest degree.

VALMONT:
You and I will go on and on.

MARQUISE:
Our story is never done,

MARQUISE / VALMONT:
Because we have found something more than love.

1.8

(They stare at each other, their gazes locked. Valmont moves slowly toward her, his mouth coming to meet hers. She smiles and turns.)

MARQUISE:
So how can you refuse my command?
Enlighten me, I don't understand.
This woman you're pursuing is a silly little prude.
And she's your latest interlude?
Who'd believe it!
Tell me briefly, what are your plans?

VALMONT: An artist's plans are never brief. But mine are already in motion.

Yesterday, I met the lovely creature.
She was strolling in the garden
With my aunt when I arrived.
It was quite a pleasant surprise.

1.9

The scene transitions to the gardens of the Château Rosemonde. Tourvel is strolling in the gardens, as before. Slowly, and slightly out of breath, Madame de Rosemonde enters, escorted by her maid, Adelaïde.

ROSEMONDE:
   There you are, dear girl,
   I might have known.
   Always I can find you in the garden.

TOURVEL:
   Madame de Rosemonde,
   How are you this morning?

ROSEMONDE:
   Like the others, I suppose.
   Heaven knows,
   When you've lived as long as I,
   You grow thankful by and by
   To have made it through the night
   And be feeling just all right.

   Still, this fresh air does me wonders.
   I'm beginning now to understand
   The reason why you pass the days outside.

TOURVEL:
   Have I been neglecting you, dear friend?
   That was never my intent.

ROSEMONDE:
   Of course not, child.
   I'm glad to see your time so happ'ly spent.

   The gardens are here to be enjoyed,
   So enjoy them.

TOURVEL:
   So I do, and I always have.
   Something in a garden is very close to God.
   Quiet, still, and innocent,
   Beauty so unflawed.

   Simple in its splendor,
   Modest in its grace,
   It's so easy to surrender
   To this quiet, perfect place.

(Rosemonde's major domo enters.)

MAJOR DOMO:
Madame, the Vicomte de Valmont has arrived.

ROSEMONDE:
Then bring him, by all means, bring him.

(The major domo bows and exits.)

Madame,
You remember that my nephew,
The Vicomte de Valmont,
Was due for a visit today.

TOURVEL:
Oh yes, I remember.

ROSEMONDE:
Well then, listen to what I must say.

His reputation no doubt precedes him.
And yes, it's probably more or less true.
He follows anywhere vanity leads him,
And who can say the things he might do.

Still, we must not judge him too harshly —
His soul is not completely corrupt.
He's kind as well and he's pious (well, partly)
But yes, you'll find him a little abrupt.

TOURVEL:
Madame, let me put your mind at ease.
Yes, I know all those stories
And all these things I do recall.
But listen to me now.
I do not judge on hearsay.
No, I do not judge at all.

ROSEMONDE:
Spoken like a Christian, indeed.

(The major domo returns with Valmont)

VALMONT: Dear aunt!

ROSEMONDE: Ah, Valmont!

(They embrace. She holds him at arm's length)

(ROSEMONDE):
  Come and let me see you,
  How you've grown!
  Handsome still, and charming...
  (Seeing Tourvel)
  Beg your pardon.

  Madame de Tourvel,
  The Vicomte de Valmont.

VALMONT:
  Madame de Tourvel,
  A pleasure to meet you.

TOURVEL:
  Likewise, monsieur,
  I've heard so much about you.

VALMONT:
  Indeed?
  Well, don't let that frighten you off.

TOURVEL:
  Monsieur, what do you mean?

VALMONT:
  No doubt you've heard the tales
  About my shameless past.
  And yes, I must admit
  That most of them are true.
  I've had my share of wine and wench
  And hidden rendezvous.

TOURVEL:
  Then is this a confession?
  It seems to me that proves
  Your heart is in possession
  Of feelings of repentance,
  And with each modest sentence
  Your wicked ways improve.

VALMONT:
Would you be my confessor, then?
Your husband would not approve.

TOURVEL:
My husband is in Burgundy.

VALMONT:
How sad that is for you.

ROSEMONDE:
(Motioning to Adelaïde for assistance)
I hate to interrupt your chat,
But darlings, I must take my nap.
So for now, I bid you both adieu.

The day is for the young who have the strength to stay awake and enjoy it. Until dinner, my darlings.

(She exits, steadying her steps by taking Adelaïde's arm. Smiling, Tourvel and Valmont watch her leave.)

TOURVEL:
Your aunt is such a dear.

VALMONT:
I know.
Her heart is cast in gold.

TOURVEL:
Perhaps we'll find a bit of her in you.

VALMONT:
You're far too bold.

(Laughing)
I do believe you are trying to convert me.

TOURVEL:
I have a friend who'd say that
That would be impossible,
Who told me I should stay as far
Away from you as possible.

VALMONT:
  Oh, indeed?
  And who might that be?

TOURVEL:
  You know I cannot say.

VALMONT:
  And still, you think you could convert me?

TOURVEL:
  It would be a great achievement,
  And a challenge, I confess.

VALMONT:
  But would you try it, truthfully?

TOURVEL:
  You know the answer's "yes."

1.10

The lights fade on Tourvel as she exits. Lights rise back on the marquise, who is on her upper platform. Valmont is caught in a spotlight, and Tourvel fades back into the darkness of Valmont's memory.

MARQUISE:
  So are you to be a priest?
  Valmont, I see it now!
  You'll rise above the squalor,
  As clerical as your collar —
  Upon which is your leash, held by that girl.

VALMONT:
  (Moving to rejoin her)
  I'm not the only one.

From what I understand, Belleroche has been your only lover for entirely too long.

MARQUISE: Jealousy becomes you, but it is hardly appropriate.

VALMONT:
   If he were just one of many
   I wouldn't complain in the least.
   But since he's not, I am certain
   I can serve more than a priest.

MARQUISE:
   You, you and I
   We have our separate paths.
   But if you are willing...
   I have a deal to make.

(MARQUISE):
   Come back to Paris when you've won your little game.
   And then one night of passion with me you can claim.
   But I'll require proof.
   It must be written proof.
   Some sign of her affection, of her shame.

VALMONT:
   Why do we have to play this game?
   Reward me now, it's just the same.
   What kind of proof?
   I should have known.
   A means to damn the girl to shame!

MARQUISE:
   You know me well...
   Valmont, is it a deal?

(They drift apart once again, continuing their written responses.)

VALMONT:
   A night with you in exchange for her reputation?
   I'd be a fool to refuse!

MARQUISE:
   Keep me posted then of your work,
   Until the deed is done.
   Now I must rest,
   This letter's gone on far too long.

(The lights fade on the marquise. Valmont turns to face the audience.)

VALMONT:
Ahead lies a path full dangerous moves.
Step out of turn and you're certain to lose.
Playing with fire, don't dare turn away,
For hearts will be won and broke in a day.

1.11

Shift to the marquise's salon. The lights rise on Volanges, Cécile, and the marquise, already in the midst of tea and conversation.

VOLANGES:
Then the comtesse said she smelled
Revolution in the air...
How absurd! What a silly idea!
It's clear to see
The world is as the world should be.

(They laugh as a servant refills their cups. For a moment, there is a knowing look on the servant's face.)

MARQUISE:
It's so nice to spend some quiet time
Engaged in conversation
Which has no urgent news to pass,
No dire information.

VOLANGES:
Ah, this wine so scrumptious and sweet!
I'd better slow down till after we eat.

(The maid Victoire enters, whispers something to the marquise.)

MARQUISE: Excellent! Show him in, Victoire.

At last! Our final guest has come.

(Victoire shows in M. le Chevalier Dançeny, a young musician.)

Cousins, may I present to you
The Chevalier Dançeny.

Dançeny, my cousins, Mme. de Volanges and her daughter, Cécile.

DANÇENY: *(Bowing to Volanges)*
It's an honor, madame.

VOLANGES: Likewise, young man.

DANÇENY: *(To Cécile)*
And mademoiselle, I am charmed.

CÉCILE: *(Dumfounded)*
Oh...yes.

(There is an awkward silence. The marquise cuts in.)

MARQUISE: I met him at last night's opera. He gave the most exquisite discourse on Lully's "Isis and Galatea."

VOLANGES: You're a music lover then?

DANÇENY: Yes, I am. It's what I do, actually. I Teach. Music, I mean.

(The women look at him expectantly. He stumbles, not accustomed to carrying the conversation.)

Yes, I teach heart... I mean harp, yes, that's it. I teach harp ... and the claveçin...

MARQUISE: Charming. He knows what he teaches.

VOLANGES:
    Oh, you do? Then it's fate.
    For my daughter was taking
    A lesson or two at the convent.

CÉCILE:
    Yes, it's true.
    And I'd like to be learning again.
    I've a harp of my own in our parlor.

MARQUISE:
    What a splendid notion!
    When will coincidence cease?

VOLANGES:
    At last, she'll be happy! —
    And maybe give me some peace.

DANCENY:
> Do you know many pieces already?

CÉCILE:
> No, no, just a few simple songs.

DANCENY:
> We'll have to change that.

CÉCILE:
> Yes, yes, I'd like that.
> I'd like that a lot.

VOLANGES:
> Then it's set! Now shall we eat?
> It seems we're in for quite a treat.

MARQUISE:
> Yes, the table is set as well.

DANCENY:
> With food for a king, I'd say by the smell.

MARQUISE:
> Oh good, monsieur, you brought your appetite.

DANCENY:
> Oh yes.

MARQUISE:
> *(Aside)*
> Well, there's plenty around to sate it tonight!

(Volanges, Cécile, and Dançeny exit. The marquise turns to the audience.)

> At last! What bliss!
> Though fate had been a bit remiss.
> I've found the key at last in this ungainly boy.
>
> He's at the age
> When every glance becomes a crush.
> He'll take the girl without a blush.
> It's in a word, sheer perfection!

(She heads out after the others. Blackout.)

1.12

A gunshot. Lights come up on Valmont outside the Château Rosemonde, pointing a smoking rifle at the audience. A quartet of hunters stands off from him with their hounds, polishing their muskets. Valmont remains facing the audience, his valet, Azalon, nearby.

VALMONT:
Forgive the lateness of this letter, madame,
But this time I really have good reason.

HUNTER 1: *(Beckoning)*
Valmont!

VALMONT:
(As he joins the others)
It's not that I'm not missing you...I am.
But we're now in the midst of hunting season.

HUNTERS:
Thank God for the rustic life!
How rare is the task I'm now confronting.
What more could a man request,
But a perfect day for even better hunting!

(Tourvel appears. She calls Valmont over to her.)

TOURVEL:
You weren't at mass today, monsieur.

VALMONT:
I'd other things to do.

TOURVEL:
You hunt each morning, so you say.

HUNTER 1: Valmont!

VALMONT:
Madame, I must be on my way...

(The men move off with Valmont, who remains slightly apart from them. Tourvel sends a servant after Valmont. She then exits.)

(VALMONT):
How distrustful she was of my morning excursions,
She didn't believe where I went.
And soon I was followed by one of her servants.
It was quite an auspicious event.

I learned all of this from my servant,
Who's bribing and bedding her maid.
With the beds and the prying
And everyone spying,
Success is a whisper away.

HUNTERS:
Thank God for the rustic life!
How rare is the task I'm now confronting.
What more could a man request...

HUNTER 1:
But maybe wine and women after we're through hunting!

HUNTER 2: Are you going to desert us again today, Valmont?

VALMONT: What?

HUNTER 3: Yes, always sneaking off in the middle of our excursions.

VALMONT: I usually hunt alone...

HUNTER 1:
Of course it is, in truth, a woman he is hunting!

VALMONT: No, really...

HUNTER 4:
Thank God for a moment's rest!

HUNTER 3:
How grand are the sunny days of summer!

HUNTER 1:
Before we go further on...

HUNTER 4:
We'd best break out the wine to get a little numb-er!

(The men laugh, unpacking a carafe and glasses. As they pour, Valmont moves off from the others, motioning to Azalon, who follows. Tourvel's servant follows them.)

VALMONT:
And so, I went off alone.
I let her servant follow close behind me.
And when he would get too close,
I'd turn my back and fire,
Albeit somewhat blindly.

(He fires his rifle again, sending the servant reeling.)

I led him on a merry chase,
Down a path I'd preconceived.
We reached a village I had found,
And a family in need.

1.13

The scene shifts to outside the small shack belonging to M. LaPierre. A tax collector and his impounders are in the process of confiscating the family's belongings.

VALMONT: I'd selected the perfect family: A man, woman and their three boys on the brink of ruin. They couldn't pay their taxes and were about to lose everything. Thus the stage was set for my hidden audience…

LAPIERRE:
Please, monsieur, have mercy upon us.
We're hungry and we've nowhere to go.
Please, if there's a God up above us.
He would save us from this fate…

VALMONT:
Just a minute.

What is this?
How dare you treat a man like this!
This ends right now, you must desist.

TAX COLLECTOR:
I can't do that, monsieur.

VALMONT:
   If payment is in question...
   Take this and go!

(He tosses the tax collector a bag of coins.)

MME. LAPIERRE:
   God bless you, monsieur.

LAPIERRE:
   You've saved us with your kindness.
   Your truly heaven sent.

(They kneel before Valmont. He opens another bag, and gives out some coins.)

VALMONT:
   They knelt at my feet with grateful wonder.
   I gave them a few more coins.
   How strange is this feeling to help another.
   It has its own naïve appeal.

LAPIERRE:
   In God's image we are made,
   By your word we have been saved!

(Tourvel's servant rushes off. Valmont remains, his face amused, but also contemplative. Fade to black.)

1.14
INCIDENTAL: "CÉCILE'S SECRET"

Shift to the Volanges salon. Cécile sneaks in, uncovers her harp. There she removes a letter from between the harp strings. She reads it quickly, then turns, clutching it to her breast.

1.15
I FOUND A LETTER

CÉCILE:
   Do I look different today? I feel I do.
   Maybe it's the way I walk,
   The way I hold my head,
   The way I laugh at absolutely nothing.

If I seem so 'come-what-may', I guess I am.
If I could convey this change,
I'd say it all began
The day I found the world between my harp strings.

When your life is nothing but bricks and walls
And books and notes and scribbles,
You think you know all there is to know,
You're above all childish quibbles.

It is, you say, that life is such,
And no one could know any better.
But then you find your world is changed — surprise!
By unsealing a letter.

I found a letter!
Where one would least expect it.
I found a letter!
It was small and perfect,
The ink was smudged just a bit,
But still the name was clear.
Dançeny, I have your letter here.

(She heads back in the direction of her room.)

It's not every day that a girl receives
A love note from her teacher.
And some would say that the girl would be
In the wrong to let the boy reach her.

But what one hears is not what's seen,
So who is to say what's accepted?
Perhaps it's best to say one thing
And then do the thing you rejected.

I found a letter!
Between the A and B strings.
I'll write a letter…
But it could be wrong…
No, it can't be wrong! Yes, it could!
So why am I thinking of…
Dançeny, I think we are in love!

(Back in her room, she sits at her desk happily, discovers another letter, and tears it open. It's from the marquise.)

MARQUISE:
Let me be the first to give one warm wish,
A toast to your engagement.
Though you don't know yet, your maman has set
Quite a prosp'rous, if tired, arrangement.

Your future lies with the Comte Gercourt,
A prize, though old and accruing.
He drools, they say, in his sleep — oh well!
He has teeth enough when he's chewing.

Congratulations, my dear girl!
Please don't tell your maman
That I've spoiled her surprise.
Let it be our little secret.

(Lights fade on the marquise and a very stunned Cécile.)

1.16

Shift to the terrace at the Rosemonde estate. Sitting with a letter, Tourvel looks up as Valmont returns from hunting.

TOURVEL:
Here you are at last, monsieur.
You must have caught a forest full of game.
You were gone so long.

VALMONT:
My luck, I'm afraid, was in short supply today.

TOURVEL:
Oh come now, monsieur.
You needn't be so modest.
I know what you've been up to.

VALMONT: What do you mean?

TOURVEL:
My servant this morning
Was handling an errand
In the village nearby,
He was passing through there when
He saw you.
He saw them,
The family that you saved.
Monsieur, you saved them!

You paid their taxes, yes it's true.
You gave them love with every sou.
They will prosper thanks to you.
What a wonder, what a joy
To see you in our Lord's employ!

In His image we are made,
And by His grace we all are saved.
Sir, your work will be repaid,
For the righteous and the good
Will find both peace and brotherhood.

VALMONT:
You mustn't make so much out of nothing.

TOURVEL:
It isn't nothing, monsieur.

VALMONT:
Well then, I suppose my game is up, madame.
You've found me out — now what?

1.17
TOURVEL:
(Taking up the letter, perusing its contents.)
How can it be true
That one with such good intentions,
One such as you,
Has earned a reputation
For a life of depravation?
How can good be an extension
Of amoral dedication?

VALMONT:
Ah, madame, you see me through extremes.
Though I am a man of many means,
I'm a long way from sinner,
A long way from devil.
The truth is lying somewhere in between.

TOURVEL:
And so this reputation
Is an undeserved creation?

VALMONT:
No, but partial fabrication
By a party you won't mention.

(He attempts to take the letter she is holding. She pulls it away)

My intentions aren't mine alone,
They're mostly imitation
Of other people that I've known,
Of current situation.

But now a new star guides my sail.
In you my darkness gives way to light.
God prevails.
Day has come.
I end my journey with the night.
A new life has begun!

(He takes her by the shoulders and meets her eye to eye.)

One cannot see the face of God
Without knowing His holy cause.
You are the vision that I see.

(She resists him, unknowingly dropping the letter.)

Ah, see how my weakness grows.
I swore I wouldn't let these feelings show.
Oh, hear me and help me to be free.

TOURVEL: *(Softly, distraught)*
No.

VALMONT:
How did I let this weakness grow?
I swear I tried to let these feelings go.
Please, hear me and help me to be free.

(Tourvel rushes off. Valmont takes a moment, then picks up the letter, which she has left behind, and reads.)

"I have witnessed his games of deception..."
"Valmont can never be changed..."
(Turning the page, looking for a signature)
"...Madame de Volanges!"

(Blackout.)

1.18

Lights rise on the Volanges salon. Volanges and the marquise are at a table, playing cards. Cécile sits at her harp. Dançeny is seated at the harpsichord.

DANÇENY: That was very nice, Cécile. Exercise number 12, once again. This time quicker still. After four: 1, 2, 3....

(He begins a rhythm on the harpsichord, Cécile joins in. The marquise picks up the deck of cards.)

MARQUISE:
Shall we play again?

VOLANGES:
Well, if you insist.

MARQUISE:
(Aside)
The way that she plays, who could resist?
(To Volanges)
Deal the cards.

(To Cécile)
Darling, I'm moved.
How your playing's improved overnight.
(To Volanges)
The chevalier must be a wizard.

VOLANGES:
(Dealing cards)
He is. Now let's see...
What are trumps, twos or threes?

MARQUISE:
No, no, trumps are the queens.

VOLANGES:
Oh, that's right.

I must confess, Dançeny's priceless.
He's nothing less than a genius.

MARQUISE:
Yes dear, he's good.
But my dear, if you would...
(Volanges plays a card.)
Are you finished?

VOLANGES:
Finished.

MARQUISE:
Really?

VOLANGES:
Really!

MARQUISE: Good.

(The marquise plays a card and takes the trick.)

Then why don't we listen to this next piece,
Did I mention it's my favorite?
I chose it.

1.19

THE GAME

(She nods to Cécile who begins to play. Dançeny and Cécile keep their eyes on each other. The card game continues as Cécile sings.)

CÉCILE:
> Love is just a game,
> And by its name we weave
> The tallest of tales,
> We regale countless make-believes.
>
> Shall we two begin?
> Let's take a spin with chance.
> My hand in your hand,
> Let us whirl until the world joins in our dance.
>
> Close your eyes,
> Let us ride this merry-go-round
> That flies us to someplace grand,
> Where stars light the seas
> And the trees are golden.
> We can hold on to the clouds above the land.
>
> Come play in my dream,
> Where life can seem untamed.
> Don't wait, for it's late,
> And my heart is crying out to start the game.

1.20

(As the music ends, the marquise takes a final trick. Dançeny rises and moves to stand at the door.)

MARQUISE:
> Well, I've won again!

VOLANGES:
> Yes, you always do.

MARQUISE:
> It's just that I know a trick or two.
> *(Turning to Cécile)*
> Dear Cécile! ...

VOLANGES:
> *(Parodying the marquise)*
> (Well, I've won again!)

MARQUISE:
Darling, you play like a master.
How fast you have learned.
(To Volanges)
Dear cousin, our Dançeny's waiting.

VOLANGES:
He is? He's a gem!
Quite a noble young man.

MARQUISE:
And his methods are certainly firm.

VOLANGES:
Yes, as I was saying,
Nothing compares to his playing...

MARQUISE:
Cousin, you're keeping him waiting.

VOLANGES:
(Not understanding)
Waiting?

MARQUISE:
(Softly)
Pay him.

VOLANGES:
(Realizing)
Pay him!

MARQUISE: *(Under her breath, rolling her eyes)*
God!

VOLANGES:
(To Dançeny)
Darling, come and we'll see to your fee.
My head's in the clouds so pay me no heed.

(Volanges and Dançeny exit. The marquise sits with Cécile.)

MARQUISE:
Cécile, what do you think of Dançeny?
Is he the maestro that he seems?

CÉCILE:
Madame, I need your true discretion.
After every music lesson,
I feel like my soul has touched the sky.

It's Dançeny, he writes to me
And tells me of a secret love,
A love without which he will surely die!

Could that be true?
What should I do?
I know that I'm betrothed,
And yet I loathe to think
I haven't yet replied.

Madame, I've always trusted you.
I need to know what I should do.
I feel my heart is bursting, tell me why!

MARQUISE:
Tell me, dear Cécile, do you love him?

CÉCILE:
He's all I ever see when I dream.

MARQUISE:
I think I know a way you can write him.
Just bring every note to me,
So I know they're what they seem.

CÉCILE: *(Hugging her)*
I love you!

(Volanges returns with Dançeny)

VOLANGES:
Then from England we sailed on to Spain.
Of course, in the end, it had to rain.

MARQUISE:
(Standing)
Well, now I must leave.
I believe it is late.

VOLANGES:
You don't have to go.

MARQUISE:
(Stopping Dançeny, who is leaving.)
No, chevalier, wait!

Would it be imprudent of me
To ask you to walk with me home?

DANÇENY:
Certainly not!

MARQUISE:
Then let us depart!
(To Cécile)
Until I next see you,
Adieu, and be true to your heart.

(They bid good-bye.)

1.21

Cécile and Volanges disappear from view as the marquise and Dançeny move into the street. They laugh and talk, eventually arriving at her château.

MARQUISE:
What a lovely time.
You have the Midas touch.
In three weeks she's improved so much,
(Giving him a playful curtsy.)
Chevalier!

DANÇENY:
I must give credit where it's due,
My teaching her is thanks to you.
And she has the finest talent.

MARQUISE:
Yet, you seem sad!
Oh, my poor chevalier,
I know now the cause of your sorrow.
But if you are brave
And will heed what I say,
Cécile will be with you and soon.

DANÇENY:
  Madame, you don't understand!
  It's not what it seems!
  I'd never allow dishonorable thoughts...
  I never would dream....

MARQUISE:
  Of course you wouldn't, silly boy.
  That's the only reason I've agreed to help you.

  My cousin is a gem to me,
  I want to see her happy.
  She says she wants to be with you.
  How could I then deny her?

  Tomorrow night, I will take Cécile's mother to the opera...alone. Cécile will stay home, and I've arranged for the servants to be dismissed early. Be at the Volanges estate at seven sharp. Cécile will be waiting there for you.

DANÇENY:
  Oh madame, is it possible?
  I have dreamed, dreamed of that night!
  If there is a way to repay...
  I'll do anything!

MARQUISE:
  Just be there on time.

DANÇENY:
  I will be, I will be.

MARQUISE:
  Just be true to your word.

DANÇENY:
  Oh, thank you again!

MARQUISE:
  I want you both happy,
  So go now and dream of your love.

1.22

Shift to the gardens at the Château Rosemonde. Her Bible on a nearby stone bench, Tourvel cuts fresh flowers with her maid Julie. They chat and laugh together.

TOURVEL: Oh, Julie, this one's beautiful! Look.

(Valmont enters, looking for her. Bothered by his approach, Tourvel hands the last of the flowers to Julie and dismisses her.)

These are enough. Take them back to the château.

VALMONT:
There you are madame, I might have known.
Once again we meet here in the garden.

TOURVEL:
Monsieur de Valmont, what is it you wanted?

VALMONT:
Just to see you, I suppose.
Heaven knows.

You've become as scarce as gold.

TOURVEL:
For good reason, I am told.

VALMONT:
Is the truth so wrong to tell?

TOURVEL:
This won't do, monsieur, farewell.

(She tries to leave. He stops her.)

VALMONT:
Perhaps I overstepped my station,
But silence finally had to give way.
Inspired by your beauty,
Enforced by your virtue,
They gave me the strength to finally say:

I'm in love, desperately in love,
But I cannot hope for a thing I cannot have.

All I ask of you then,
All I dare to wish,
Is for you now to teach me,
To tame this too full heart of mine.
What's wrong with such a...

TOURVEL:
How did I once believe
You'd show respect for me?
I was warned...

VALMONT:
How can you still not see
My complete respect for you.
Once I knew you...

TOURVEL:
Come now, let's be frank,
I still see through you.
Clever words, but empty,
You don't know me.

Your feelings offend,
That is all I can say.
You'd do well to forget them,
Keep silent and still.
It's what I would have you do.

VALMONT:
If that's what you want, then so be it.
You see, in this I'm a slave to you freely.

TOURVEL:
Monsieur, if that is true,
And if you want what's best,
I have for you one more request.

VALMONT:
Anything.

TOURVEL:
If you'll do as you say,
Then monsieur, go away.
Leave this house, and return now to Paris.

VALMONT:
　So I will, without pause,
　Without reason or cause.
　But I beg two small things.

TOURVEL:
　No, there is no room for deals now,
　When honor is at stake.

VALMONT: I only ask what I, in my own small way, deserve. Someone has wronged me in your eyes. I'd like to know who...

TOURVEL: No, my confidence is sacred. If you respected me, you wouldn't ask such a thing.

VALMONT: Then at least let me write you once I leave. A harmless correspondence...

TOURVEL:
　No more games
　Deft and quick.
　No more wordplay,
　No more parlor tricks.

　It cannot be revealed
　That we're in correspondence.

VALMONT:
　And it won't be, I assure you.
　And my letters will contain nothing to offend.

TOURVEL:
　Then all right, you can go.
　And my letters will show
　That it's reason, not hatred, that guides me.

VALMONT:
　Bless you madame, you have saved me.
　I take you in my heart.

(*He leaves. Tourvel remains, her mood distracted. She sits on the stone bench, tries to read and cannot. She closes her Bible and goes back to the château. Fade to black.*)

1.23

A darkened stage. The marquise appears.

MARQUISE:
How many the fools in the world, vicomte.
I think I know each one.
One or two I'm related to.
Just hear what they've recently done!

I had the perfect plan to get
Our two young lovers alone.
But when I arrived at my cousin's estate,

(Volanges appears, lights reveal her salon. Cécile is standing anxiously at a window nearby.)

She said I should go out...

VOLANGES:
...alone.

MARQUISE:
Alone?

VOLANGES:
Alone.

I've been feeling so ill you see.
It must be something I ate.

MARQUISE:
Perhaps you shouldn't have eaten.

VOLANGES: What?

MARQUISE: I mean, perhaps you should watch what you eat.

VOLANGES:
I try, I try.
But these days it seems
Like everything gives me trouble.

(Cécile motions for the marquise. She has seen Danceny coming up the walk.)

(VOLANGES):
  I plot and I plan,
  I skimp and I weed,...

(The marquise makes a vague gesture to Cécile, just as Volanges turns to her, and she lets the gesture slide into some fiddling motion with her garments. Volanges continues.)

  ...And try not to heed the urge to indulge,
  (I don't want to bulge)
  But now this I'll divulge:

(Dançeny knocks. The marquise stomps her foot on the floor and slaps at an imaginary insect.)

MARQUISE: Mosquitoes. Terrible this year.

VOLANGES:
  (Turning away, continuing)
  ...When sweets are around then I have to concede.

(Dançeny starts to knock again.)

CÉCILE: *(Spying him through the window)*
No!

(Volanges is startled, and stops again, turning toward them. But the marquise sits Cécile down, as if telling her a wicked secret, and they both cover the outburst by laughing at the imaginary jest.)

MARQUISE:
  (To Volanges)
  Did I mention the reception after the show?
  The host is the baker, Monsieur de Mareaux.

VOLANGES: That handsome baker?
  (Standing, grabbing her shawl)
  Isn't it amazing how quickly a sickness can go?

MARQUISE: Astounding.

(Heading for the front door, they pass Cécile on the way out. The marquise, opening the door, sees Dançeny and slams the door in his face. She lets out a small laugh.)

Could we perhaps go out through the back way?
I would love to stroll out through your garden.

VOLANGES:
Oh yes,
That would be nice.
I've quite a green thumb
If you need my advice.

1.24
INCIDENTAL: "THE FAN"

They leave. Cécile lets Dançeny in. He bows, she curtsies. She turns shyly to lead him into the salon. Volanges is heard approaching from offstage, ad libbing something about leaving her fan. Dançeny ducks behind a screen. Volanges and the marquise reappear. Cécile snatches up the fan and hands it sweetly to Volanges, who kisses her. Dançeny pokes his head out from behind the screen. The marquise gestures for him to get down.

1.25

(The marquise ushers Volanges toward the exit.)

MARQUISE:
Madame, we might miss the first act.

VOLANGES:
Then let us be off.

Though if we have missed it, what matter?
There's bound to be more.

(They leave. Dançeny emerges timidly. In his fear, he has crushed the blossoms he brought for Cécile. He offers them to her.)

DANÇENY:
These were for you, mademoiselle.

CÉCILE:
How nice.

1.26
IF ONLY

(She takes the flowers and sits on the divan. He sits on the opposite side. They sit. An awkward silence ensues. Dançeny sighs.)

DANÇENY:
Look at her sitting there.
She glows with a light of her own.
I want to speak,
And yet I don't,
So together we still are alone.

Something makes me tremble.
There's so much here we could win.
But then we could lose,
So how do I choose?
I don't know where to begin.

If only she'd make the first move,
Save me from having to choose,
If only she'd say the first word,
I'd live for her,
I'd give to her
All of the songs yet unheard.

CÉCILE:
Look at him sitting there,
As bright as a clear summer sky.
I want to speak,
And yet I can't.
I don't even know how to try.

Something keeps me silent.
It scares me to think he might leave.
But what should I do?
I haven't a clue.
I don't know what to believe.

If only he'd take the first chance,
Smile and ask me to dance,
If only he'd break the silence,
I'd go to him,
I'd show to him
The tend'rest and truest romance.

CÉCILE / DANÇENY:
Yes, we could be warm if only...

CÉCILE:
He'd build the fire we need.

CÉCILE / DANÇENY:
Safe in his/her arms if only...

DANÇENY:
She'd offer them,

CÉCILE:
He'd offer them,

CÉCILE / DANÇENY:
And with them a warm guarantee.

DANÇENY:
But what if she told me no?

CÉCILE:
But what if he means to go?

CÉCILE / DANÇENY:
What if I'm dreaming?
What if I'm seeing
More than what really is there?
How could I dare?

Oh...

DANÇENY:
Save me from having to choose!

CÉCILE:
If only he'd take the first chance,
I'd dance with him!

DANÇENY:
   I'd dance with her!

CÉCILE / DANÇENY:
   For then I'd have nothing to lose.
   Oh, if only...

CÉCILE:
   If only I wasn't so scared...

DANÇENY:
   If only I knew that she cared...

CÉCILE:
   If only I saw something there...

CÉCILE / DANÇENY:
   Oh, if only...
   If only I dared.

(They remain apart. Slow fade to black.)

CD2

2.1

The marquise's salon. She sits, shaking her head at the outcome of the preceding scene. Valmont suddenly storms in. She sits up.

VALMONT:
   Cécile Volanges must be ruined.
   Do you know why?

MARQUISE:
   (Motioning to a seat for him near hers)
   Of course. Gercourt...

VALMONT: No.

   I was sent away.
   Forced to go away by the creature I adore.

MARQUISE: Adore?

VALMONT:
But do you know who
Was the one whom advised her thus?
That horrible shrew,
Your cousin, Madame de Volanges.

MARQUISE:
And so our knight returns from his crusade,
And having lost the war,
Now seeks satisfaction in lesser trade.

VALMONT:
I have not lost!
No, far from it.

(Sitting down in the seat)
Madame de Tourvel is still within reach, you see...

I obeyed her only on certain conditions.

One's which she'll find impossible to fulfill.
If she will:

One, let me write to her and answer in turn.
Two, give the name of my accuser.

Then I would go,
Then I would know
She would be true to her word.

MARQUISE:
(Standing up, walking away from him)
How ridiculous!
And yet you've returned.
Why?

(She moves to an easel, and casually flips through a pad of drawings.)

VALMONT:
Why?
Because I've learned, madame, I've learned.

She cannot keep the conditions I gave,
And so I am free to return when I may.
And when she reads the letters I send,
Her heart will ignite a fire within.

(VALMONT): In the meantime…

Paris is ripe with love.
Sweet, unsuspecting love.
A little rose is blooming,
One that needs my grooming.

MARQUISE:
One that needs your touch, such as it is.

VALMONT:
(Moving to her)
One might turn to two…

MARQUISE: Who?

VALMONT:
Maybe you…

MARQUISE:
(Breaking the mood, moving across the room to sit on a divan)
I have no need for a crutch.
As for Cécile…

Dançeny's been a catastrophe,
A master of music,
disaster at love.
The two were alone.
Four hours alone!
Not one little kiss.
And with all my assistance,
He failed to insist.
Persistence to morals
Just shouldn't exist!

VALMONT:
So you see, men are complex creatures.
Much more than you thought.

MARQUISE: Complex in their stupidity.

VALMONT: Here's a thought:

(VALMONT):
(Crossing to sit down beside her on the divan)
When love first comes,
It comes as a surprise.
And often unidentified as love at all.

The heart pounds,
The hands shake,
The tongue trips,
And tries to catch up.
The voice sounds,
But words quake,
And love stalls,
But make no mistake.

Love so young can be inflamed.
It simply needs some walls to climb.
Give the boy an aim,
A hindrance or two,
Then see how he'll do.
But then I think it's past its time.

MARQUISE:
(Suddenly showing greater interest)
Oh now, vicomte, not with your aid.
You could be our chevalier's advisor.
Use lies or truth to push him along.

VALMONT:
But if he's not any use to us,
I'd waste my time.

MARQUISE:
Leave that to me.
I've had a thought.
I think I'll go see Madame de Volanges.

VALMONT: Which reminds me...

(Standing up, offering his hand. She takes it and also stands.)
My aunt, the saint, has asked me
To extend an invitation to your cousin,
The Gorgon of France.

MARQUISE: Your aunt certainly likes a full house, doesn't she? Good. That works in well with my plans.

> Good-bye, vicomte.
> Sup well, and think on future obligations.
> Entrust your aunt's request to me.
> Now I'm off to destroy a romance!

(She exits, leaving Valmont to ponder her words. He smiles, shaking his head, then follows. Fade.)

2.2
MERTEUIL'S RECITATIVE

A darkened stage. A tight spot comes up on the marquise, who reappears opposite of where she last exited.

MARQUISE:
> I went to see Madame de Volanges,
> To put in place so perfect a plan.
> Our pupil needed hindrances,
> That much now was clear.
> Well, I would give him hindrances,
> Never fear it!
> All the cards were now in my hand.
>
> Start very simply,
> Strike the smallest spark,
> All of your actors
> Ache to play their parts.
> This one shall be my masterpiece!
>
> Mother, daughter, foolish lover—
> With this visit, all will suffer!

2.3

The music takes her to the salon of Volanges who greets her happily. The marquise responds with distress.

VOLANGES:
> My dear friend!

Your visits always brighten my day!

MARQUISE:
　Oh, if only that were so.

VOLANGES:
　You seem distressed.

MARQUISE:
　I am, madame, I am!
　And rightly so.
　May I sit down?

VOLANGES:
　Of course, of course.
　Now, tell me what's the matter?

MARQUISE:
　(Sitting)
　It's poor Cécile.

VOLANGES:
　Please, tell me what you mean!

MARQUISE:
　I will, but where do I begin...?

　I'm afraid Cécile and the Chevalier Dançeny
　Are engaged in a dangerous correspondence.

VOLANGES:
　Nonsense!
　I'm sure you're mistaken.

MARQUISE:
　I wish that I were.

VOLANGES:
　But how do you know?

MARQUISE:
　Cécile and I have grown quite close,
　You know that I adore her.
　But then lately she's not been herself.
　I think I know the reason.

(MARQUISE):
>One day when she was at her desk,
>I saw her with a letter.
>And in an open drawer were more,
>And guess who was the sender.

I didn't mean to pry, but I couldn't help glancing at the letter.

>Simple and bold,
>White traced with gold,
>From a nameless admirer.
>Then at the end, in a similar pen,
>A name for that shameless conspirer.

VOLANGES:
>Oh no!

MARQUISE:
>Oh yes!
>You can guess...
>The letter was from Dançeny!

VOLANGES:
>What a cruel twist of fate,
>Oh my darling I hate to be rude
>But I must see my daughter.
>
>You've been too good a friend.
>Sometime soon we shall spend
>Many happier moments together.
>
>All my years of living
>Never prepared me for this.
>Adieu...
>Please excuse me...
>What a nightmare this...

MARQUISE:
>*(Rising to go, then turning)*
>Oh, before I go!
>There was something else.
>I'm sure that there was something else...

VOLANGES: Oh, my God.

MARQUISE:
> Now I recall,
> And it's not much at all —
> Madame de Rosemonde's invitation.
> She wants you to come for a visit...

VOLANGES:
> How nice.
> But not in the midst of this crisis!

MARQUISE:
> Of course not!
>
> Oh, my dear,
> I hope you will forgive me,
> Bringing you such news.

VOLANGES:
> There's nothing to forgive.

MARQUISE:
> Then good-bye again.
> Until I next see you,
> My prayers will be with you...

VOLANGES: Amen!

2.4
INTERLUDE: "LETTERS"

The marquise leaves, satisfied. Returning home, she rests easy in her boudoir as, in Cécile's room, Volanges bursts in on Cécile, moving quickly to the desk drawer where she discovers the letters. She wields them in Cécile's direction, Cécile collapsing in tears. The marquise smiles broadly.

Act I–Part 2

2.5
If He Were Here

The lights rise fully on the marquise, dissolving from Cécile's room, indicating the time shift. As the marquise continues, she moves to her salon, where two letters are waiting on a tray on the tea table.

MARQUISE:
When I awoke,
I found two notes.
And can you guess who were the senders?
One from Cécile,
One from maman,
And both were begging my advice.

Irony was never richer!
Yes, I would console,
As a goddess who will switch her
Advice to suit opposing sides,
And thwart the prayers of any who confides.
How perfect!
Watch and learn…

(Suddenly, Volanges bursts in on the marquise who sits up with feigned surprise.)

VOLANGES:
Madame, you were right!
Madame it is true!
All those awful things you said are true!

I still had my doubts,
How could I be without?
But I know that what you told me now is so.
It's just as you said,
In the desk by her bed
Were the letters from that debtor's Romeo.

Who ever would have thought this could happen?
That Danceny could be such a fiend?
I'll send my daughter back to the convent.
For disaster would have struck
If you hadn't intervened.

MARQUISE:
I think that course of action May be just a bit extreme.
Your daughter's fall from grace is not the hardest to redeem.
If just this once your motherly advice to mine concedes,
The freshness of the country air may be the thing she needs.

It'd be no fuss...

VOLANGES:
The country air?

MARQUISE:
If I recall, Madame de Rosemonde...

VOLANGES:
Invited us!

MARQUISE:
And once you're there,
Your daughter's heart will grow less fond.

VOLANGES:
Distance weakens loves desires,
And restores the brain!
Regain the senses love retires.

MARQUISE:
Distance weakens loves desires.
She'll have time to
Regain the senses love controls.

VOLANGES:
(Moving off as she sings)
At a distance,
Dour resistance,
Like a sinner, has to fall.
The perfect solution for all!

MARQUISE:
And with that set,
Within the hour
The daughter, like the mother, came to call.
The perfect solution was...

(Volanges exits as Cécile bursts in on the marquise.)

CÉCILE:
Madame, you must help!
Madame, I am lost!
If you cannot help me I'll be lost!

How I've no clue,
But maman somehow knew
Where my letters from Dançeny were kept.
She's taken them all,
And when he came to call
She told him to go, oh how he wept!

(Collapsing at the marquise's feet.)
Please tell me I'm asleep and I'm dreaming!
Or show me where's the star that I crossed.
And if there is no hope in believing,
Tell me, how can I go on,
Knowing everything is lost.

MARQUISE:
I know it is a shock but you must wipe away your tears.
There isn't time for weakness now so put away your fears.
If troubles brew, try not to stew
on things you cannot change.
Instead, make cheerful phrases
and let words relieve your pains.

"If he were here."
Four simple words.
But in them lies a sort of magic.

If he were here…

CÉCILE:
I'd hold him close…

CÉCILE / MARQUISE:
And never think to let him go.

CÉCILE:
He would kiss me…

MARQUISE:
Would you let him?

CÉCILE:
Maybe once or twice!

MARQUISE:
Just enough to entice…

CÉCILE:
Time would hurry…

MARQUISE:
Not to worry!
If he were here…

CÉCILE:
Oh, if only…

MARQUISE:
Here in your arms…

CÉCILE:
Arms around me.

MARQUISE:
And think how fast the days would change to years!

CÉCILE / MARQUISE:
How lovely!
With him here.

(Cécile and the marquise laugh and hug as Volanges comes into view in her salon.)

CÉCILE:
> If he were here,
> We'd take a walk
> Down every alleyway in Paris.
> If he were here,
> We'd never talk,
> We'd never have to speak again.

MARQUISE:
> If he were here,
> You'd take a walk
> Down every alleyway in Paris.
> If he were here,
> You'd never talk,
> You'd never have to speak again.

VOLANGES:
> If that boy were here,
> I would run him down
> Every alley in Paris.
> If that boy were here,
> He would not come 'round here again.

CÉCILE:
> Softly strolling hand in hand.
> It's my only wish.
> Who's for missing modest wishing?

MARQUISE:
> Softly strolling hand in hand.
> It's a lovely wish.
> Who's for missing modest wishing?

VOLANGES:
> I would wring his neck with my bare hands!
> It's a wish I hope to see come true one day.
> Who's for missing modest wishing?

(During the final exchange of the song, Cécile and the marquise embrace and Cécile leaves, finishing the song outside.)

CÉCILE:
   It passes time,
   And soothes the heart,
   And so I'll say until the day he is near,
   "Oh, if he were here!"

MARQUISE:
   It's not a crime.
   So, what of it?
   And soon you'll see the day
   You can say, bright and gay,
   "Oh, he's finally here!"

VOLANGES:
   Wishing does it!
   In the country we'll be happy,
   Knowing he's nowhere near!

2.6

The lights go out on Cécile and Volanges and rise on Valmont, who stands on the platform adjacent to the marquise's. She smiles at him and he joins her.

MARQUISE: Everything is in place for you, vicomte. Both Cécile and Mme. de Tourvel under one roof. And what's more, Mme. de Volanges has seen fit to invite me along. She says I work miracles with her daughter.

VALMONT: Then it seems we should travel together. How lovely.

(Kissing her hand)
I'll be able to claim all three of my prizes at practically the same time.

MARQUISE:
   (Suddenly angry)
   You'd better watch yourself,
   Your words are out of line.
   I won't be numbered with those fools,
   I'm not their kind.

(MARQUISE):
　Make sure you understand,
　Don't ever be confused,
　I am not some whore that you can use!

(Shortly)
I won't be leaving for the Rosemonde estate right away. I have personal matters to attend to first.

VALMONT: What? Another lover?

MARQUISE: Is that jealousy I hear?

VALMONT:
　Of course it is,
　I'm still your willing slave.

MARQUISE:
　Not so willing these days.

VALMONT: What do you mean?

MARQUISE: I think you know.

(He begins to speak, she silences him with a wave.)

You need to go now. Hurry back to your aunt's.

VALMONT: And you?

MARQUISE:
　I will get there when I do, vicomte.
　Now, adieu.

(Lights fade on the two of them.)

2.7
Reprise: "Correspondences"

Lights rise on Dançeny, who comes forward, holding an envelope.

DANÇENY:
   Dear Cécile,
   I'm in torment, the distance between us
   Turns seconds and minutes to years.
   But at last I have found us a guardian angel,
   He speaks and despair disappears.

(Valmont appears on a platform above, preparing to depart.)

   The Vicomte de Valmont is our savior.
   And you know him already I hear.
   He'll deliver my letters,
   So know, when he's with you,
   Your chevalier also is near.

VALMONT:
   (Descending to stand beside Dançeny)
   I am your friend,
   And a friend who will serve like no other.
   I too have loved
   At a distance, I know how you suffer.
   Victims of fate,
   And the whims of a tyrannous mother.
   I can supply
   You the means and the chance to be free!

DANÇENY:
   He's our friend.
   When he speaks you will hear me as well.
   He is also in love, so he knows.
   He knows how we feel,
   Knows how I need you here.
   No other can help us.
   It's time to be strong.
   If we hold on
   Then we will at last be free!

(They turn. Dançeny gives Valmont the letter, and they kiss each other's cheeks. They both move off.)

2.8

The Château Rosemonde. Rosemonde sits at table with her guests, Tourvel, Volanges, Cécile, and an old Commandeur. They drink a toast as the afternoon sun spills into the room.

ALL:
  Bless the sun!
  See it shine!
  Bless the grapes upon the vine!

COMMANDEUR:
  Let's stomp them all to wine!

VOLANGES:
  Why Commandeur, you wicked man!

COMMANDEUR:
  It's true, I am an awful ham,
  But I tell the finest stories.

CÉCILE:
  Tell us one then, of adventure and love,
  (Giving her mother a glance)
  Of heartache and loss and betrayal.

VOLANGES:
  Cécile!
  Please pay her no mind,
  She just isn't herself.
  (Nudging Cécile)
  Children are never content!

ROSEMONDE:
  I'm most content with life
  When surrounded by such friends.

VOLANGES:
  Thank you for the invitation.

TOURVEL:
  I echo your elation.

ROSEMONDE:
If your daughter's heart needs lifting,
She should speak to this dear girl.
(Indicating Tourvel, who smiles at Cécile)

TOURVEL:
(Turning to Cécile)
I hear your wedding has been set.
I'm happy you are so fortunate.
I too am happ'ly wed...

(She is interrupted by a noise from offstage, the sound of Valmont approaching.)

> **MAJOR DOMO:** Monsieur de Valmont, with all due respect, please wait! Madame is at table with her guests. You must be announced. ...Oh, monsieur!
>
> **VALMONT:** Oh, nonsense! Enough of this. Look, Madame is my aunt; you are but her servant. If Madame is at table, I can assure you that I would be welcome.

(All turn to see Valmont enter, brushing past the Major Domo.)

VALMONT: *(Charmingly, with a chuckle)*
How easily they forget their stations.

MAJOR DOMO:
Madame, the Vicomte de Valmont...

VALMONT:
Yes, yes, enough of that.
I don't think I'll be intruding.
(To Tourvel)
Or am I mistaken?
(Indicating an empty seat beside Tourvel)
Has this seat been taken?

TOURVEL:
I thought you'd been called away, monsieur.

VALMONT:
Let's not talk of business now...

VOLANGES:
Valmont, how did I know?

ROSEMONDE:
I'm glad you made it back, dear.

VALMONT:
You have quite a pack here.
Is there room enough for one more guest?

ROSEMONDE:
Of course there is, my dear, no need to ask.
The Marquise de Merteuil is more than welcome.

Madame de Volanges has already told me...

VOLANGES:
There's been a delay...

TOURVEL:
(Standing)
Madame, may I be excused?

ROSEMONDE: Of course, my dear.

VOLANGES:
If you don't mind, I think I will join you as well.

VALMONT:
Let's all be sociable and follow their lead.
Shall we retire to the parlor?

COMMANDEUR:
That would be the thing to do.
(To Cécile)
By God, I'm stuffed dear, aren't you?

(The Commandeur, grabbing his wine glass, leads them into the salon. Tourvel remains a moment, eyeing Valmont suspiciously.)

TOURVEL:
You play these games too well, monsieur.

VALMONT:
What do you mean by that?

2.9
Confrontations

COMMANDEUR: *(From the salon)*
Attention, please, everyone! Attention!

(Tourvel turns from Valmont with a final glare and moves to a divan in the salon, apart from the others. She gives her attention to the Commandeur, as Valmont comes to sit in a nearby chair.)

> The muses have smiled,
> For this beautiful child
> Has asked for a tale of adventure.
> And so for a lark,
> I've a story to spark.

ROSEMONDE:
> Oh, tell us!

CÉCILE:
> Yes, tell us!

COMMANDEUR:
> Of course!

(As Valmont and Tourvel begin engaging in their own, unheard conversation, a servant brings coffee to the table where the others are situated. Waving away the coffee, the Commandeur stands, takes a sip of his wine, clears his throat and begins.)

> We start the story overseas.
> In what they call the Brave New World.
> In darkest hour.
> In times of war.
> And perils loomed on every side!
>
> I slaughtered savages in forests dark and dank.
> And from the Redcoats I won freedom for the Yanks.
> But out of all my foes,
> The hardest to depose
> Was a sweet young thing called Sarah Jane.

(COMMANDEUR):
> I fought the sea to foreign lands.
> I killed a bear with my bare hands.
> Through highs and lows,
> Who would suppose
> The girl would be my worst of foes?
> But with true love comes greater woes.

VOLANGES:
> *(Distracted by Tourvel)*
> I know that look that's in her eyes.
> When something's born, when something dies.
> When something's done,
> And then undone.
> A thing to make the angels cry.

COMMANDEUR:
> I had the notion to take Sarah for a wife.
> And then in Paris we'd enjoy the carefree life.
> And when she said, "I do"
> I knew the war was done.
> Now we live in London! Who has won?

CÉCILE:
>Without my pen and ink
>All I do is think of ways to see him.
>But how? I'm so alone.
>So now I need a friend.
>Where can I find a friend?
>Someone to soothe this lonely ache.

VOLANGES:
>A charming story to be sure.
>*(Aside)*
>I think I heard it once before.
>But how much more
>Can we endure?
>*(To the Commandeur)*
>A charming story, good monsieur.

COMMANDEUR:
>And so a warning I now give to one and all.
>In times of peril pray you don't hear cupid's call.
>Don't be foolish,
>Love is not a game to play
>When so much is at stake.

CÉCILE:
I will not bend!
My heart is mine.
My love is chaste.
So now I find
I've made my mind.
Now is not the time to be meek.

VOLANGES:
Oh dearest friend,
I see the signs,
Why must it be?
The pure, the chaste
Can be so blind.
Can I ever make you see?

COMMANDEUR:
Not to offend,
Love is a deadly wine.
Beware the taste!
Enough of that.
Now it's time for something new...
Time for adventure number two.

CÉCILE:
(To the Commandeur)
How charming.

ROSEMONDE:
How charming.

CÉCILE:
The perfect tale.

COMMANDEUR:
Shall we begin?

CÉCILE / VOLANGES / ROSEMONDE:
Number two?

COMMANDEUR:
Once in the wars with those blasphemous Moors
I spent ten days awake, in the desert I baked
With my comrades all slaughtered and gasping for water
My future as grim as my prospects were slim.

Days would blaze hot and then night would bring frost.
Hell, you'd either burn up or you'd freeze.
But that didn't stop me from singing a prayer
Up to Christ in whose name I would kill all the heathens
Believe in the Lord and in peace you can do as you please.

ROSEMONDE:
(Finally displaying her own distraction)
What's this? What's going on here?
They argue so. I fear the outcome
For this most unlikely pair.

COMMANDEUR:
Then came a dragon from Arabic legend,
A fiend of all fire and smoke!
I had only a knife...

(The Commandeur continues the tale in pantomime, as the focus shifts to Tourvel and Valmont.)

ROSEMONDE:
Words come in fervent outbursts.
What makes each one far worse,
They're spoken with the reverence of a prayer.

TOURVEL:
You broke your promise.

VALMONT:
No! No, I have tried
To show you every deference.

VALMONT:
I speak the truth now.
Love now gives me no
Recourse to honest ways.

TOURVEL:
Why do you continue
To assault my peace of mind
By speaking to me thus?

(TOURVEL):
(Lowering her voice, remembering that they are not alone)
Abandon words of love
Which you know I can't accept.
Do you want to lose my friendship?

VALMONT:
How can I accept your friendship?
Now you've turned my life around.

The man I'd been would use
Your friendship towards deceiving you.
I can't do that.
What I offer is a love so devoted,
so ardent,
Yet so respectful too.

TOURVEL:
Then you leave me no choice, monsieur...

(The others burst into applause for the Commandeur. The interruption stops the conversation between Tourvel and Valmont.)

> **COMMANDEUR:**
> I hope you liked my silly jaunt.
> I don't intend to flip or flaunt.
> I carry on of days long gone.
> I do not want to seem withdrawn
>
> **ROSEMONDE:**
> Oh no, no not the least.
> Your tales are like a feast.
>
> **VOLANGES:**
> *(To Rosemonde)*
> Seven courses longer than you'd want!

CÉCILE / VOLANGES / ROSEMONDE:
Bravo monsieur, you are the latest Marivaux.
You are as canny as Monsieur Jean Jacques Rousseau.

COMMANDEUR:
I know a thing or two of love.
It gives my tales their extra spice.

VALMONT:
(Still privately to Tourvel)
I will be constant
Though you may hate me,
Know with love you'll find
There's no room for compromise.

CÉCILE / VOLANGES / ROSEMONDE:
The next Provost!
Let's have a toast!
Here's to you monsieur, our noble friend!

COMMANDEUR:
Here's to good friends and happy days.

VALMONT:
Madame, is something wrong?
Madame, you seem so pale.

TOURVEL:
I don't hate you.
Why do you insist on making everything a conf...

VALMONT:
(Interrupting everyone)
Excuse me, somebody fetch her a cloth for her head!
She has grown quite alarmingly pale!

(The others gather around Tourvel, except for Cécile, who is delayed by her needlework.)

ROSEMONDE: Oh, my goodness, child.

VOLANGES: *(Upset, half to herself, half intended for Valmont's ears)*
Not surprising. It was just a matter of time, considering her company.

ROSEMONDE: Do you need water?

TOURVEL: No.

VOLANGES: Here, dear, take my fan.

ROSEMONDE: Shall I summon a servant? ...

TOURVEL: No.

ROSEMONDE: ... A doctor?

TOURVEL: No!

(Meanwhile, with the others diverted, Valmont tosses Dançeny's letter to Cécile, putting a finger to his lips for secrecy. Tourvel tries to control the situation that Valmont has fabricated.)

> I'm fine now.
> Give me room please.
> I need fresher air.

VOLANGES:
> You should go rest.
> That would be best, dear.

TOURVEL:
> *(Rising, distracted)*
> A stroll will clear my head.
> Please forgive this rudeness.

(She exits into the gardens. Valmont watches her go. Volanges stops in front of him with a fiercely protective glare.)

2.10
INTERLUDE: "THE GARDEN"

Transition to Rosemonde's gardens. Tourvel moves about the garden and rests on a stone bench, her hand to her chest. She tries to calm herself. She looks around.

2.11
THE GARDEN SONG

TOURVEL:
>Here among the trees,
>Among the seas of roses,
>I'm again at ease.
>How blessed these reposes.

>Sweet the columbine,
>The endless lines of clover.
>Here the sun still shines,
>The storm, I find, is over.

>Alone in the midst of a garden,
>A warden to its blooms,
>The stones and lilacs ardent
>To keep away the gloom.

>Now as shadows creep,
>The robins cheep their stories.
>Now I shall not weep,
>They'll sing to sleep my worries.

2.12

(Valmont appears, startling her.)

VALMONT: You have a lovely voice.

TOURVEL:
>Monsieur, you spat on my trust.
>You promised to go,
>You know that you must.

VALMONT: I already went.

TOURVEL:
>And yet you returned?
>Why?

VALMONT: Why?

>Because I burn, madame, I burn!

(VALMONT):
  You are the fire that scorches my soul.
  You a desire I cannot control.
  Still, I am true,
  Or is love a sin?
  And how can I tame the fires within?

  Help me persist!
  Lead me with your light.
  Don't turn away.
  Or do you pray for saints alone.
  Would you disown the night?

  Would you leave me no hope for salvation,
  Not try and lead me from temptation?

TOURVEL:
  Admit, you don't want my help.
  You drown me with lies.
  I'm wise to your ways.
  You spat on my trust.
  I do what I must!

Please go!

VALMONT:
  No!

No.

  Please, though you spurn to see me again,
  Yes, I return, and though more than a friend,
  I'll be content
  With what might have been,
  And with you control the fires within.

Please, madame, I am begging you.

TOURVEL:
  And what would you have me do?

VALMONT:
  Be my friend.
  Help me belong.
  Teach me your song.

(He sits beside her. She doesn't move. He reaches for her hand. She gives it, hesitantly, and begins her song, softly at first, then with more strength.)

TOURVEL:
(With Valmont gradually joining in.)
Here among the trees,
Among the seas of roses,
I'm again at ease.
How blessed these reposes.

Sweet the columbine,
The endless lines of clover.
Here the sun still shines,
The storm, I find, is over.

(They look into each other's eyes. He smiles. She returns his smile, her hand still in his.)

2.13
THE KEY

Back inside Rosemonde's salon. Cécile, at her needlework. Volanges, Rosemonde and her porter stand with the Commandeur at the door.

COMMANDEUR: A delightful supper, truly delightful.

ROSEMONDE: Give my love to Sarah, and have a wonderful trip back to London. And thank you for those wonderful stories. They were amazing, weren't they?

VOLANGES: Yes, simply unbelievable.

(He kisses their hands as Cécile reads from the letter hidden in her needlework. The porter escorts the Commandeur out. Rosemonde kisses Volanges goodnight, and heads off.)

CÉCILE:
(Reading from the letter.)
"At last I have found us a guardian angel…"
"The Vicomte de Valmont is our savior…"

VOLANGES: Cécile!

CÉCILE: *(Concealing the letter)*
Yes, maman?

VOLANGES: Madame de Rosemonde has retired for the evening. Perhaps you and I should follow her example.

CÉCILE: Yes,... Let me just gather my things.

(Volanges exits with a nod. Cécile takes the letter out again and rereads it. Valmont approaches, whistling a snatch from Tourvel's Garden Song. He catches Cécile trying to conceal the letter again. He stops her.)

VALMONT:
If I had been your mother,
That letter would now be ashes.
Clumsy!
You have to be careful,
If you wish to be near your chevalier again.

CÉCILE:
Monsieur, it's all that I want.
I no longer sleep,
I no longer eat, dream, sit,
Sing, sew, move, speak,
Breathe, without thinking of him.

And what does this mean,
This letter he's sent?
And will there be more?
(He turns as if to go. She grabs his arm)
Oh, dear... sir... wait... no!
Please tell!

VALMONT:
It all depends on you now.
The trueness of your love,
—if it is true—
Is what you must use to see you through this.

The letters that I bring you,
Foreseeing what we face
—the danger involved—
We must have a way of easing through this.

CÉCILE:
   I don't understand!
   The letter you brought...
   How did you...

VALMONT:
   Your Dançeny has entrusted me
   As a way to convey his words of love to you.
   (Bringing her close, in confidence)
   So be quiet now,
   I'll tell you how
   —exactly how—
   You can make our mission...

(She looks toward the door where her mother exited.)

   (Bringing her face around.)
   —Listen to me—
   Most successful, less distressful,
   Here's what you must do:

   Underneath your mother's chest,
   You'll see there trussed up with a ribbon
   Rests a hidden key.
   (Taking out a key from his jacket, Cécile looks worried.)
   Take that key with all good haste,
   Leave this one sitting in its place
   And then bring...
   —Oh now, why that face?
   You see the key you bring to me
   Allows me to unlock your bedroom door.

   From the key I'll make a copy,
   —God knows where—
   I'll take the copy,
   Give to you the one that's real,
   And then at nighttime I can steal into your bedroom.
   Then instead,
   Without risk to you or me,
   I'll bring to you the letters you adore!

(She nods and tries to move off. He stops her.)

(VALMONT):
> But before...
> Take this oil and this feather,
> Grease the hinges of your door,
> Then silence is assured.

(She nods, tries to move off again. Again, he stops her.)

> One thing more...
> Please replace with equal haste
> The key you took from mother's nook.
> For safety's sake be sure.

CÉCILE:
> Monsieur, do you think it is wise?

VALMONT: Yes.

CÉCILE:
> You're certain there's no other way?

VALMONT: I am.

CÉCILE:
> I don't want to seem ungrateful,
> So if you're sure, then so am I.
> I'll do anything that you say.

VALMONT:
> Though I truly hate deceit,
> Your chance for happiness
> Moves me in such a way,
> In this innocent affair
> — in this case —
> I will go a bit astray.

Now, go on. Maman will be waiting.

(He smiles at her. She smiles back, then exits.)

> Then with that done,
> We'll have some fun.
> I'll see you at the door!

(Lights fade.)

2.14
SHE CLOSES HER EYES

Night. On an upper platform, Tourvel sits in her room, reading by candlelight. Disturbed, she stops, recalling her lullaby to calm her.

TOURVEL:
 Now as shadows creep,
 The robins cheep their stories.
 Now I shall not weep...
 No good.

 Why am I filled with such unrest?
 For respite now I pray.
 I feel I'm treading far too deep.
 What hollow voice disturbs my sleep?

(Lights rise below on the Rosemonde salon, where the marquise sits with Valmont. The lights on Tourvel stay up.)

MARQUISE:
 How long now since I arrived?
 Four days—It feels like a millennium!
 And what have you accomplished?

 It's been a bore.
 Four uneventful days.
 And still she's given no displays
 Of burning love.

VALMONT:
 No, there you're wrong.
 She's showing all the signs.
 She's falling fast to my designs.
 You have to pay close attention.

You're angry because I haven't taken care of the Cécile matter before now. I promise you though, after tonight, you will have no cause for complaint.

MARQUISE: Good. I was beginning to have doubts about the whole affair. Still, I don't see how you think that Madame de Tourvel has any interest in you. She shows no sign...

VALMONT:
> She closes her eyes.
> Her steps fall without pause.
> Though danger gives her cause to be still,
> She moves towards me.
> I wait, she comes.
> No turning back.
> She knows, though closed, her eyes still see.

(Valmont moves as he sings, staring off, over the audience, his thoughts on Tourvel. From behind, the marquise observes him skeptically.)

MARQUISE:
> Once there was a time
> When we two were in love.
> I believe it was truly love we had then.
> Times change, you change,
> As I watch you
> Closing your eyes too.

TOURVEL:
> *(Above, from her room)*
> I have known such perfect happiness,
> Wanting what I have, no more, no less.
> Now comes a time when I want something more.
> How desire can lead us so far from ourselves!
> Once I would listen to reason so well.
> I'm already somebody else.
>
> Words are nothing now,
> Here on the edge of night.
> The path no longer clear.
> What's wrong or right, who knows?
> I pray for strength, but prayers are only words.
> What words could help me?

(TOURVEL):
  Words are nothing now
  But hopes in empty air.
  I cannot close my eyes,
  I do not dare to sleep
  When sleep brings only dreams of him to me.
  How can I not succumb to these,
  The sweetest lies,
  When I close my eyes?

MARQUISE:
  Who is falling now?
  Which one of us is blind?
  Who allows dreams of love to lead them astray?
  Who is poisoned by these lies?
  Who dares close their eyes?

VALMONT:
  She closes her eyes,
  Her hopes dissolve in air.
  Afraid to see the truth,
  She comes blind to be with me.
  She comes to these,
  The sweetest lies.
  In love, you have to close your eyes.

(They hold for a moment. Valmont and the marquise regard each other. He holds a finger to her lips; She smiles and puts a finger to his. Above, Tourvel lifts her rosary and brings the cross to her lips. Lights fade.)

2.15
INCIDENTAL: "CLOSING IN"

Cécile's room at Rosemonde's. Cécile is asleep in her bed. From the corridor outside, Valmont approaches her door, takes a key from his pocket and opens the door. He approaches her bed, observing her sleep indulgently. Cécile wakes as he sits beside her.

2.16
THE SEDUCTION

CÉCILE:
  Monsieur, what's the matter?
  My bedtime was at seven —
  You've a letter then!
  (Sitting up, expectantly)
  Give it here!

VALMONT:
  (Moving closer)
  No, I don't.
  I do bring a surprise though,
  My dear.

(He kisses her, almost violently. Shocked and confused, she struggles against him.)

CÉCILE:
  Get away from me!

VALMONT:
  Kiss me and I'll leave.

CÉCILE:
  Go, before I scream!

VALMONT:
  Who would they believe?
  A little girl?
  Please explain how I gained your key.

(He kisses her again, pressing her down on the bed. She continues to struggle.)

  Admit you enjoy it!
  Each feeling I'm arousing,
  Every heated cry
  Suits you well.
  I can tell,
  Soon you'll welcome me inside.
  Tonight you're mine.

(As her sobs grow weaker, he slips the gown from her shoulders. He strokes her hair, kissing the tears on her cheek.)

    Feel anything, every touch,
    Take a chance and lose control.

(He continues his seduction.)

CÉCILE:
    Through darkness I hear you calling me,
    And I am afraid.
    Please help me I'm falling far to fast.
    Though I try resisting,
    Something keeps insisting,
    "Do not fight."

VALMONT:
    There's no point in resisting.
    All you want, I can give.
    Wet desire so warm and so right.
    You have no need to fight.

CÉCILE :
    Filled with fear, filled with warmness,
    I will give, you will take.
    Secrets I have kept out of sight
    Bare their fruit tonight.

VALMONT:
    I'll fill you the way a man should,
    And you will change.
    Your flower will bloom to womanhood.
    Anyone so touched
    Can never be the same
    From day to night.

CÉCILE:
How can I betray Dançeny?
I pray to God
That you will understand
What I don't understand.
A little girl I may be tonight,
But who will I awake?

VALMONT:
Hold still I must taste you.
Your Dançeny would waste you,
And your maidenhood
Must be claimed by a king.
He'd never teach this song I sing
Of flesh!

(In silhouette, we see him above her, and her rising to meet him. They freeze in tableau as the scene recedes from view and transforms.)

2.17
A Simple Time

The streets of Paris. Dançeny walks along the river Seine. He comes to a bridge and looks over.

DANÇENY:
There was a simple time,
Right at the very start.
Everything was blooming,
Everything was good,
So we went on assuming
Things would stay the way they should.

There was a simple place,
Known simply by our hearts,
Free of rules or reason.
We wanted to remain
Forever in that season,
To forever stay the same.

Too late now we know,
Nothing stays constant,
Nothing stays simple,
Everything constantly changes.
But if that is so,
Even our troubles can't stay consistent,
As times quite insistently change!

So, then, the chance remains,
If we can just stay true,
One day we will find
Our trials behind us,
And thus we can start anew,
Back in a simple time.

(Fade to black.)

2.18

The terrace at the Château Rosemonde. The marquise sits fanning herself. Cécile suddenly rushes in, in tears.

CÉCILE:
Madame, you must help!
God, what have I done?
Madame, you must help!
What have I done?

(Kneeling at the marquise's feet)
I was in bed when he came like he said,
But we kissed he insist we undress.
I told him to go, and I tried saying "no,"
But the word somehow twisted to "yes."

Madame, it was Valmont, he's a monster!
I see maman was right all along.
I need your good advice, give an answer!
I need you here with me,
Now that everything's gone wrong.

MARQUISE:
(Almost coldly)
My dearest coz, I never was the kind to waste a word.
I understand he forced your hand, but crying is absurd.
The shame of love is like its pain, you only feel it once.
And once it's past, within your grasp
comes all that you could want.

CÉCILE:
Don't you understand?
Look what I have done.
I don't think I can
Escape the web he's spun.

MARQUISE:
Little fool!
Look inside your self.
There you'll find the strength you need.
You have gained a key and a tool
Worth the sacrifice.

CÉCILE:
I was scared, but I felt alive.
And I paid his awful price.
I can't play this game.
I'm a fool!
I don't know the rules.

MARQUISE:
Look back at the song I gave you.
Heed its advice.
The lesson it gives is worth the price.
It's all about surviving,
Constantly revising every rule.

(Suddenly gentler, she strokes Cécile's hair. Cécile rests her head in her lap.)

MARQUISE:
Rules, there are no rules.
And that's a rule I make.
You can't get ahead being steadfast,
For rules will break.

(Lifting Cécile's chin)
Use the gifts you have,
And dear, don't be ashamed.
With men as your enemies,
You must be most ruthless in this game.

CÉCILE: Nothing makes sense anymore.

MARQUISE:
You have the chance for happiness that very few can find,
The happiness of freedom and security combined.
To have this marry Gercourt without protest or complaint.
And when you're wed you'll be unchained
from motherly constraint.

Cécile, don't you see what it is to be free,
To pursue any moment of pleasure?
And Valmont you'll find, in his own little way,
A charming and valuable treasure.

CÉCILE:
I never wanted all these things that have occurred.
But in the darkness somehow everything was blurred.
And what of Dançeny?
How can you be so sure?
I don't even know what I've become!

MARQUISE:
You have to play the hand your dealt.
Enjoy the pleasures that you felt.
He'll love you more.
Just be assured.
You'll seem an angel in his eyes!

MARQUISE:
Your feigned indifference will appease your dear maman.
And Dançeny will find resistance admirable.
He'll find you twice as pure,
And you'll be held in awe.
Husbands, lovers, you can have them all!

CÉCILE: But what about Valmont?

MARQUISE:
Tell me, could you like being with him?

CÉCILE:
(Seeking the marquise's approval)
I see how it could come to be nice.

MARQUISE:
Let him come again then, and listen.
Learn from him what you can.
Now then, that is my advice.

(The marquise kisses Cécile, stroking her hair as the lights fade.)

2.19
FINALE: "SECRETS"

A spotlight rises on Rosemonde standing center stage, surrounded by darkness.

ROSEMONDE:
Secrets!
Tonight is the night for telling secrets!
Tonight is the night for selling lies!
The eyes won't reveal what is there to steal
As the sunlight dies.
Secrets!

(The lights rise suddenly on the rest of the stage, revealing a crowded gala. From the crowd, three women become prominent, gossiping.)

OLD WOMAN:
Did you hear the brave vicomte
From the Château de Lamont
Recessed with the Comtesse de Drieux?

YOUNG PRUDE:
Mon Dieu!

GIDDY WOMAN:
It's true!

OLD WOMAN:
They had a little rendezvous.

It was quite the tidy scam
Till her husband forced their hand!

GIDDY WOMAN:
He broke in on their repose
And he broke the vicomte's nose!

OLD WOMAN:
I hope there'll be a duel!

YOUNG PRUDE:
Well, there should be,
That's the rule.
Swords a-lashing!

GIDDY WOMAN:
Wounds a-gashing!

OLD WOMAN:
Fist's a-flying!

YOUNG PRUDE:
People dying!

GIDDY WOMAN:
Oh, what a nice little duel it would make!

YOUNG PRUDE:
Now, for the comtesse I don't feel.
She shouldn't try to double deal.

OLD WOMAN:
She's really much too greedy.

GIDDY WOMAN:
Well in men we all are needy!

(The other two stare at her, scandalized.)

(Embarrassed, correcting herself)
Well... some of us, that is.

(Tourvel enters. The three women catch sight of her and begin to chatter quietly. Their eyes, as well as the eyes of the other guests seem to follow Tourvel as she moves through the room.)

TOURVEL:
Whispers are there in the evening hours,
Whispers that speak of a love's avower betrayed!
Afraid to be heard in the sting of their words,
They ply their trade in whispers.

(The whispering grows louder as she moves through the crowd. She suddenly finds herself face to face with Valmont.)

VALMONT:
Secrets!
You think that these people are speaking secrets,
You know that their eyes are seeking you,
Undoing your mask, though they dare not ask
If you love me too.
It's a secret!

(He approaches her. She retreats. They are swept up in the crowd. Volanges, with a friend and Cécile, suddenly appear.)

VOLANGES:
As I told my dear Cécile,
We must all watch how we feel,
And love with a coveted ease.

FRIEND:
You tease!

VOLANGEES:
Oh, please!
I learned this from the dear marquise.

Moderation is a must,
Not in fortunes, but in lust!
Trade passion to cash in —
Adjust!

CÉCILE: *(To herself, as she wanders from her mother)*
Adjust?

How can I adjust?
If I could just be strong
To leave you behind,
But I find that my heart's too fond.

Love is all I want,
But then, why Valmont?

(The crowd dances, then parts, revealing Tourvel and Valmont dancing together. They mix with the crowd which parts again, this time revealing Valmont dancing with Cécile. Volanges moves to cut in. When Valmont accepts, Volanges drags Cécile away. The crowd sweeps the stage again, singing.)

CROWD:
Secrets!
Tonight is the night for selling secrets!
Tonight is the night for quelling fires!
The liars and saints
Will show no restraints
As the truth retires,
Secrets!
As the day expires,
Secrets!
Then the nighttime sires secrets!
etc.

(The chorus builds, then suddenly freezes in time as the marquise appears at the top of the staircase. She oversees the crowd as if a chess game.)

MARQUISE:
Once again the game has begun.
Once again I am the one who has won.
Before me a king will turn to pawn.
For I see every liaison!

(She begins descending the staircase, and gesturing here and there toward various couples, which spring to life and seem to move on strings that she manipulates.)

There's no move I cannot contemplate.
I do not hesitate
To give my check a mate,
To bait my prey with secrets!

(The entire crowd begins dancing to her words. She stops on a middle platform halfway down the staircase. As she continues singing, Tourvel, Valmont, and Cécile also become prominent.)

(MARQUISE):
   I gain every goal by saving secrets.
   In vain every soul is craving mine,
   The tiniest sign of how I design,
   How I intertwine secrets!

TOURVEL:
   Whispers!
   Whispers are there in the evening hours,
   Whispers that speak of a love's avower betrayed!
   Afraid to reveal
   What it is that I feel,
   I now am keeping secrets!

CÉCILE:
   How can I betray
   Dançeny? I pray,
   I must keep this secret!

MARQUISE:
   Secrets...
   Secrets...
   Everyone is keeping secrets!
   Secrets...

VALMONT:
   Secrets!
   Do you love me too?
   Do you love me too?
   Secrets!

TOURVEL:
  Do you love me too?
  Do you love me too?
  Do you love me too?
  It's a secret!

CÉCILE:
  How can I be true,
  Danceny, to you?
  I must keep this secret!

MARQUISE:
  Secrets...
  Everyone is seeking secrets!
  Secrets...
  Everyone has a secret!

VALMONT:
  Secrets!
  You think that my eyes are keeping secrets,
  My heart, is it really seeking you?
  Be true, did you say?
  Will you let me stay?
  Do you love me too?
  It's a secret!

Intermedio

2.20
Prelude

2.21
Reflections

Darkness. Slowly, a special rises on the marquise who sits at a vanity facing the audience. We can see her face through the empty frame of her mirror. She admires herself.

MARQUISE:
  A splash of rouge.
  A small stroke of the lash.
  A careful dab and then a flash
  Of red...
  And white...

  The slightest touch
  Removes the telltale line.
  It takes an artist to refine
  And build the perfect reflection.

  Reflections all around us,
  So simple.

  But in these images is a power
  And a purpose so profound.
  What is life but what is seen and understood?
  What is good?
  Is it real?
  Or just another sorry preconception
  Of a God I've never seen?
  It all depends on what you see.

  And if you control the things you see,
  You control your own life.
  And if you control what others see,
  You control theirs.

I realized this a long time ago,
When life was ready to unfurl
Before a simple little girl.

(A scene opens up of the young marquise with her mother, moving through Paris society. The marquise observes from the side.)

As a child I learned early to smile,
While the world threw at me many, many words.
Words such as...

(The socialites and the mother sing as if lecturing the young marquise.)

SOCIETY WOMAN:
Modesty!

SOCIETY MAN:
Obedience!

PRIEST:
Chastity!

MOTHER:
Silence!

MARQUISE:
I smiled!
And as children often are,
I was ignored.
And my mother thought...

SOCIALITES / PRIEST:
Modesty!
Obedience!
Chastity!
Silence!

etc.

MOTHER:
Ah well, the child is bored.

MARQUISE:
She didn't know.

(MARQUISE):
  As a child I learned early to see,
  As I hid within the silence of my age,
  Past all the...

SOCIETY WOMEN:
  Modesty!

SOCIETY MEN:
  Obedience!

PRIEST:
  Chastity!

SOCIALITES / PRIEST:
  Silence!

MARQUISE:
  ...I saw!

  All the secrets all around me,
  Past virtues meant to confound me,
  And past the words:

SOCIETY WOMAN:
  Modesty!

MARQUISE:
  Ridiculous!

SOCIETY MAN:
  Obedience!

MARQUISE:
  Absurd!

PRIEST:
  Chastity!

YOUNG MARQUISE: Chastity?

MARQUISE:
  Well, I was young!

Some things were still beyond my comprehension!
But this I surely knew:
Secrets lived in those around me,
And in those secrets power too.

And so I grew...

(The scene fades back to the marquise at her mirror, where her preparations are slowly progressing.)

A steady smile,
A penetrating glance,
A measured calm and that helps enhance
The whole facade...

It takes a will
To mask your every thought,
To keep your inner secrets caught
Behind the perfect reflection.

I learned these things a long time ago,
When life was waiting to be seen
By a girl of just fifteen.

(The scene shifts to the young marquise, and to a trio of girls her age, among others, being chaperoned at a dance. The girls whisper at each other behind their fans as boys their age pass.)

    Fifteen!

YOUNG MARQUISE:
    Fifteen!

MARQUISE / YOUNG MARQUISE:
    What a perfect age!
    An age of...

MARQUISE:
    Powder!

YOUNG MARQUISE:
    Perfume!

MARQUISE / YOUNG MARQUISE:
    And love!

MARQUISE:
But what is love?

YOUNG MARQUISE:
What is love?

THREE YOUNG GIRLS:
What is love?

GIRL 1:
Love is winks!

GIRL 3:
Love is drinks!

GIRL 2:
Love is wine!

GIRL 1:
Love is whispers in the darkness
In these secret little houses!

THREE YOUNG GIRLS:
Love is fine!

Love is music!
Love is air!
Love is candles!
Love is dare!
(The boys leading the girls to the dance floor)
But most of all, loving means dancing!

(They all dance a minuet around the stage, as the marquise watches.)

MARQUISE:
Yes, it was entrancing!
Still, there had to be more...
In those whispers, in those houses...
What did women do?

I thought I knew, but had to be sure.
And what better place to learn of sin
Than in the halls of God?

(The scene shifts to a church where the young marquise arrives for confession. In the confessional beside her sits the priest, covertly sipping communion wine.)

    I went to confession with the usual words...

YOUNG MARQUISE:
"Forgive me father for I have sinned."

PRIEST:
And tell me child, what is this sin?

YOUNG MARQUISE:
I have done...

PRIEST:
Yes?

YOUNG MARQUISE:
I have done...

PRIEST:
Go on, go on...!

YOUNG MARQUISE:
I have done everything that women do!

(The priest suddenly coughs up a sip of wine, spilling the remainder on himself. Sputtering, he stands, bumping his head painfully against the confessional, and begins to lecture the young marquise.)

MARQUISE:
It was a lie!
But his reaction was such that then I knew —
I wanted to do the things women do!

(The young marquise steps forward out of the scene, looks back at the frantic priest, tidies her skirts a bit, and sets off on her way.)

    What is love?
    What I learned
    Is it isn't at all for pleasure.
    What is love?
    It's a tool
    Meant for more than just leisure.

(MARQUISE):
I realized this that day in the church,
And life was ready to explode!
But then I reached home...

(In the scene, lights rise on the mother, who is waiting with an older gentleman, M. le Marquis de Merteuil.)

And found I was to be...

MOTHER:
Married.

YOUNG MARQUISE:
Married?

MOTHER / MARQUIS:
Married!

(As the lights fade on the scene, the mother, in pantomime, introduces the Marquis to her daughter.)

MARQUISE:
You can imagine my shock.

I was of the age, but never had I thought...
Ah well, it was for the best.
And so in a virginal wedding bed,
I learned what love is!

And my teacher, the dear marquis,
He was so sweet, so very considerate.
He taught me all he knew,
Then promptly expired,
And as a widow I retired to the country.

You may wonder why I am writing this letter at all, vicomte.

I want you to understand where we stand...

Reflections,
Take a moment to heed them.

For in these images is a danger
And a darkness to be found.
As a widow I learned faster than before.
To reflect is nothing less
Than to respect yourself.
And give pause,
reflecting on cause,
And in turn to the effect that's made
By affecting and directing what is seen.

Just imagine your life as a woman.
Any word can be your ruin,
Any thought can be your undoing.

And so...
Year after year,
Stroke after stroke,
Smile after smile,
Lie after lie,
I took control.

And when I returned to society,
It was as actress and author,
And love would be my art!
What was love to me now?
I wanted not to feel it,
But to feign it, to arouse it.
That was my call.

Never too easy to please,
But never to unrelenting.
A person who stumbled a bit,
But always worth repenting.

Men would come.
I would receive them.
Men would leave and if they told,
Who would believe them?

I put myself out of reach,
Made friends of the most devoted,
Using them for defense.
This rule I quickly noted:

(MARQUISE):
   I never write, no proof is left.
   And so that I would never fall
   Under anyone's control, I made a vow:
   I would not wed.
   I would not bow
   To anyone's call.

   And can you blame me?
   Can anyone blame me?
   I survive, I don't apologize,
   I don't look back, I move on!
   Surely, you can understand.

   You...
   You, my nemesis.
   You, my confidante.
   You, my greatest of friends.

   You, I wanted before we met.
   You, my opponent, but don't forget,
   You are good, but I am better.
   Read this letter and take it to heart.
   What I want I will get.
   Whom I hate, I'll destroy.
   If I have to employ the devil himself,
   I'll do it without regret.

   And who can blame me?
   You can't blame me!
   And neither can anyone else!
   For if they had the strength,
   They would do the same!

(Blackout)

Act II

2.22

The Storm

Nighttime at the Château Rosemonde. A few weeks after the end of Act One. The sound of thunder echoes through the halls. Lights come up on Cécile who, from her bed, stares out a window at the rain.

CÉCILE:
When your life is nothing but naps and walks
And lunches with your mother,
And you need to find something new, something soon,
Or else you're likely to smother,
The days drag on without relief,
And nothing to pass as a pastime.
Then quite by chance your world is changed...
(A knock at the door)
By a knock in the nighttime.

(Cécile opens the door. It is Valmont. She pulls him in, kissing him passionately.)

VALMONT:
Cécile, you are learning.

CÉCILE:
I have the finest teacher.

VALMONT:
Girl, you flatter me.

CÉCILE:
Well, I try.
Come inside.
(Climbing onto the bed, pulling off her nightgown)
I've been practicing my lessons.

VALMONT:
I'm sure.

(He climbs into bed with her. She strokes his hair, teasing him.)

CÉCILE:
No more a schoolgirl!
Not shy unless you wish it.
No silly schoolgirl.
I know secret names,
And obscure techniques,
For a kiss you don't need mistletoe.
Come to me, I'll show you what I know.

(She pulls him on top of her as the lights fade on them. A soft light comes up on Tourvel in her room, reading through several letters by candlelight. The storm can be heard outside.)

TOURVEL:
They're only letters,
No more than ink and paper.
No more than letters...
So why,
Why do I feel like I'm on the brink
Of some great misfortune?

(She puts the letters away in a desk drawer. The lights dim on her considerably, but not entirely, and we can still see her shadow as the scene shifts. Elsewhere, a match is struck. Valmont lights a candle, Cécile asleep behind him. As he speaks, he casually laces up his shirt and shoulders into his coat.)

VALMONT: Dear Marquise: Five days have now passed since your departure, and I am acutely aware of your absence. The storm, which moved in on the day you left, has still not abated. And the garden strolls with Madame de Tourvel, to which I have become accustomed, have all but stopped.

(He begins to move as Tourvel gets up and begins to roam with her own candle. As Valmont continues, their movements carry them about the stage, their paths circling each other, never yet intersecting.)

Five days the rain has fallen,
Five days trapped inside.
Ah well, there are things to keep me occupied.
And while I do enjoy the little girl on the side,
She's beside the point.

(Having seen her mistress leave her room, Julie cautiously approaches Tourvel's desk. From another drawer, she removes a different bundle of letters, conceals them, and leaves the room.)

> Five days, the storm is building,
> Five days, no relief.
> And hell, the tension builds beyond belief!
> And now I roam the empty halls like a thief!
> A brief recess...

(A crash of thunder. He and Tourvel nearly collide. She gasps, then lets out a nervous laugh.)

TOURVEL: Oh Monsieur, you startled me.

VALMONT: Likewise. You're up so late.

TOURVEL:
> It was the storm,
> It rages so, I couldn't sleep.

VALMONT:
> Nor could I.

(They stare at each other, each gauging the other's thoughts. Tourvel finally breaks the gaze.)

TOURVEL:
> We had best get on to bed.
> Good night, monsieur.

(She tries to move away. Valmont grabs her arm. She turns from him.)

VALMONT: Why are you running from me again?

TOURVEL:
> Why do you ask me to put it in words?
> You know why I do!
> Please don't press me to say things we'd only regret.
> Let me remain true!

(He suddenly takes her in his arms and kisses her. She pushes him away, slapping him hard.)

> Do you want me to hate you,
> Is that what you're after?

(He pulls her in again and kisses her. She slaps him again with greater force. He puts a hand to his face.)

(TOURVEL): Why are you doing this?

(Again, He pulls her in. She raises a hand, but it wavers, trembles, then moves to his cheek, bringing him in closer. They kiss passionately, then she pulls away abruptly. She moves from him, crying, her voice breaking. He approaches slowly behind her.)

> **(TOURVEL):**
> Please monsieur, I am begging you,
> If you love me as you say…
> I have no more strength,
> Let me be,
> Leave me to my grief!
>
> **VALMONT:**
> I cannot deny the things I feel,
> Neither can you.
> No more can we make polite refrains.
> One more step before us,
> One we can't ignore
> One to end our grief.

(He carries her through the door to her boudoir and lays her on the bed. She makes no moves of protestation. He begins to undress her.)

TOURVEL:
Please, monsieur…
Please, monsieur…

(He doesn't answer.)

Do it then.

(He hesitates.)

Why are you waiting? This is what you wanted!

(He pulls away, his back to her. She lets out an agonized scream. Valmont clutches his head to shut it out, then lets out a similar scream. He rushes into the hallway, where Julie has appeared.)

VALMONT: You! Go get my aunt! Your mistress is ill!

(Running past her, heading offstage)
Did you here me? Go!

2.23
INTERLUDE: "TOURVEL'S DESPAIR"

Julie goes to fetch Rosemonde as Valmont exits. Tourvel pulls herself up and begins to frantically gather her things. She throws a shawl across her shoulders. She stumbles, then collapses back onto the bed in anguish.

2.24
Julie returns with Adelaïde, who quickly pushes a wheeled chair carrying Rosemonde, her hair covered and wearing a sleeping gown. They rush into the room.

ROSEMONDE:
   Poor child! What is this?
   What has happened?

TOURVEL:
   Oh madame, my heart is torn.
   I have to leave,
   I have to leave now!

(Rosemonde bobs her hand toward Adelaïde, dismissing her. Adelaïde and Julie both leave the room and sit in the corridor.)

   And yet to leave him
   Is the last thing I could want.
   Madame, it is Valmont,
   I am in love with him!

ROSEMONDE:
   Oh, my dear,
   I fear I knew that this was coming.
   I fear I knew the pain that was in store.

TOURVEL:
   How?
   How could you know?

CD 3

3.1
THE NATURE OF MAN
ROSEMONDE:
When autumn comes, my dear,
And you're as old as I,
When winter's frost draws near,
You'll know the reason why,
Why love is never easy,
Why a woman's heart must break,
Why the nature of man is not to understand,
But to take all he can take.

Leave well enough alone.
You're better on your own.
Escape now if you can,
From all that is called man.

The nature of man is not to nourish,
The nature of man is war.
He lives for conquest,
Best when killing,
That's what he was created for.

How can women like us
Know the reasons for his schemes?
He, a slave to the whims of his lust,
We seek tenderness in dreams.

A woman knows how to love another,
She'll give all she can and more.
She lives to nurture,
Search her feelings,
That's what she was created for.

There can never be peace
When two so different touch.
Once entwined there can be no release,
Words have never mattered much.

Fickle are the seasons!
Fickle is a man!
Exquisite in his treasons.
Don't try to understand the reasons
Why the summers die,
And autumn gives way to winter
Without hint or any meaning.
There's no meaning in the ways of men.

The nature of man is not forgiving,
But if he's released you, go.
Say farewells quickly,
Leave no warning,
And forget the love you know!

Prudence, my dear,
You will know when.

TOURVEL:
I cannot ever be near him again!

3.2
INTERLUDE: "TOURVEL'S DEPARTURE"

Tourvel gathers some things, hugs Rosemonde, and exits. As she leaves, the scene recedes from view.

3.3
VALMONT'S RECITATIVE

Outside the Château, in the midst of the storm, Valmont rushes back onto the stage.

VALMONT:
She is gone! She is gone!
What a fool I was to show her my mercy.
She left like a thief in the middle of the night,
Out of sight! Out of sound!
But the consequence will be her own destruction.

(VALMONT):
   I was so close!
   She took advantage of my kindness,
   For I pitied her,
   Her eyes so blue,
   Stained with tears,
   All her fears opened up for me to see.
   Oh, the vulnerability...
   It was so seductive!

   But now is past a time for pity,
   Now with Love and Vengeance acting as one.
   I'll bring her to her knees,
   I shall see her shaken by the storms,
   Storms that now have shaken me.
   I shall be victorious and free!

3.4

The marquise appears on the opposite side of the stage, holding a letter. At the sound of her voice, Valmont turns his head to look at her. As he listens, he gradually moves to a neutral area, opposite the marquise.

MARQUISE:
   Dear Vicomte, don't be maudlin.
   What did you expect the poor
   Woman to do but depart?
   Once she finally surrendered
   And still wasn't taken,
   Her pride took control of her heart.

   You must learn how to improvise better,
   To create ways of reaching your goals.
   You rely on your methods
   While I create new ones;
   Seduction for me is an art.

(They turn and face each other across the gap of empty stage.)

VALMONT:
   You, you and I,
   We once saw eye to eye,
   Now it would seem that we don't agree at all.

Why is that so?
Could we have changed all that much?

MARQUISE:
Maybe it has something to do with love.

VALMONT:
It's not enough that she give in to me.
I have to own her completely before I am free.

MARQUISE:
Vicomte, it's just as I've heard!
The rumors are true!
What's happened to you?

VALMONT:
What is it you've heard?
What rumors are those?

MARQUISE:
It is said that you are sick with love.
Some have guessed the reason
For your lengthy absence.

If you value your reputation at all, you will forget this affair and come back to Paris immediately.

VALMONT:
Let them talk.
When I do return,
I will put them all to shame.
When I've claimed my prize,
And my proof,
Then they will toast my name!

Then you and I can reclaim our past.
Don't forget the deal that we made.
And I'll prove to you
I was never in love.

(Blackout)

3.5
INTERLUDE: "SUNSET"

Dusk. Tourvel's boudoir at her home. The last strains of sunlight seep through the window. Tourvel sits in a chair, staring at nothing, a Bible and a soup bowl on the table beside her. Julie enters. Reaching for the bowl, she finds it untouched and gives her mistress a worried glance. Tourvel waves the bowl away. As Julie removes it and leaves, Tourvel notices her Bible and attempts to read. But distracted, she retrieves a letter hidden near her heart and unfolds it. Then, casting it aside, she puts her face in her hands. Again taking the letter, she tears it up. Noticing the sunlight, she stands, assuming a blank resolve. She moves to the window and gazes out at the setting sun.

3.6
SEASONS RUNNING FROM OURSELVES

TOURVEL:
(Drawing the curtains)
Let the sun fade away,
Let the night fill the day
Till the shadows and silence have claimed me.
With the moon as my guide,
I'll be lost in her light,
Silver rays my disguise.
Blinded to the truths that surround me,
Safe from memory!

When we find reason fails,
We spend seasons running from ourselves.
Masquerades
Privately played
Deep in our minds,
We stumble to avoid dancing with temptation.

Day shuns night with regret.
We may fear love but we can't forget.
Memories burn,
Passions return
Soothed by the night,
When dreams turn all concern to soft intoxication.

But the night isn't quite the companion it seems.
Dreams aren't our friends.
Though in light black and white are so perfectly clear,
We're blinded when darkness descends.

Summers fly, winters pass.
Like the seasons, feelings never last.
Like lovers who,
Always untrue,
Seek in their time
To leave and thus undo all of the trust you gave them.

Why did he have to be waiting there in the rain,
So painfully near?
Is he there waiting where I could find him again?
Oh, when did this love first appear?

Run away! Far away!
Love's the word that you must not say!
Leave all behind,
Cold and resigned!
Winter has come again.
Spend seasons running blind without a heart to run to.

3.7

(Valmont appears out of the darkness. She doesn't notice him at first.)

VALMONT:
So this is how it must be,
The two of us?
Eternally separated,
Yet joined in unhappiness.

TOURVEL:
(Startled, spinning around.)
Monsieur, what are you doing here?
You have to leave.

VALMONT:
You left me no choice.

You were the first to resort to the use
Of shadows and nighttime.
You ran away from me!

(VALMONT):
   Didn't you? Didn't you?
   It was me!
   Wasn't it? Wasn't it?
   Why do you wish me unhappy?

TOURVEL:
   I only want your happiness!
   How could I not want your happiness?
   Please, you must go!
   You know that this is killing me!

VALMONT:
   I forever am dying as well.
   Forever without you,
   Death can be my only comfort.

(He reaches out for her. She turns from him. He becomes suddenly fierce.)

   (Starting to leave)
   And so to my comfort I go!

TOURVEL:
   Monsieur, what do you mean?
   No, you can't leave!
   (Struggling to block his path, he struggles against her)
   I won't let you!
   I won't let you!
   Please!
   Oh God, I love you!

(She falls into his arms. He holds her as she weeps. She raises her head and meets his gaze, wiping tears from his cheek and giving him a broken smile.)

   How could you not believe
   I'd want your happiness,
   When it's all I'll ever know?
   (Growing frightened)
   Oh God, I am so lost.
   Please help me find my way.

VALMONT:
   There are times when God cannot give you
   The comfort you need.
   Believe me, I know.
   Still, in those times,
   There's a place you can go.

3.8
A Heart to Run to

VALMONT:
   When you need a heart to run to, run to me.
   When the heavens hold no answers, I'll be there,
   Showing you there's a heart to run to,
   One you can depend on any time.
   If you need a heart to run to, run to mine.

TOURVEL:
   By loving you, will faith become
   Impossible to keep?

VALMONT:
   Our love can build a brighter trust
   That's just as strong and deep.

TOURVEL:
   Now I have a heart to run to waiting near.
   And I have a love to cherish, he is here!
   Perish the thoughts I had of running,
   Running's not the answer, it won't do,
   Unless the path down which I'm running leads to you.

VALMONT:
   All the nights I've wasted...

TOURVEL:
   All the prayers I've said...

VALMONT:
   All the lives I've tasted

TOURVEL / VALMONT:
   Were never really real at all,
   Just whispers on my bed!

TOURVEL:
> So many thoughts,
> So many words,
> So little right for speech.

VALMONT:
> But newer thoughts
> And better words
> Are now within our reach!

TOURVEL:
> And I have a heart to run to!

VALMONT:
> Any time!

TOURVEL:
> And I have a love to trust in!

VALMONT:
> Here in mine!

TOURVEL / VALMONT:
> Don't hold back the things you feel.

VALMONT:
> Give in to me completely, let me know
> That I have a heart to run to, a place to go.

(They embrace. As passion overtakes them, they move to the bed.)

> The dice are cast,
> But don't regret,
> Just keep your eyes ahead.

TOURVEL:
> The pain that's passed
> I now forget,
> I leave the tears unshed.

TOURVEL / VALMONT:
> I have a heart to run to any time,
> I have a heart to run to and he's/she's mine!

(There is a passionate moment as the lights fade.)

3.9

The marquise's dressing room. The marquise sits at her vanity, her maid, Victoire, sitting on a small stool beside her, assisting her with preparations for bed.

MARQUISE:
Victoire,
You're such a villain!
Do you really find my stories so engaging?

VICTOIRE:
Madame,
If you'd be willing,
I would sit about and hear them out for hours.
Please, just one more?

MARQUISE: Well, then. But how about something new? I just remembered a delightful parable that was once told to me by my nurse. How did it begin? Ah, yes…

3.10
THE LIONESS

MARQUISE:
In a kingdom far away
Lived a lion and his lioness
And both were brave and beautiful,
Both hunters fierce and strong.

But one day when they were stalking
Through the heartland of the wilderness,
Somehow they separated,
Somehow something went wrong.

Both found their prey with equal ease,
But there their story parts.
For the lion hesitated,
He let himself be bated
By a zebra's lovely stripes.

(MARQUISE):
>They hypnotized the lion
>And he stayed until he died.
>But the lioness was different.
>She would not be so fated —
>She ripped out her zebra's heart!
>
>And then back to home she flew
>With the swiftness of the hummingbird,
>And there she learned her husband's fate,
>She now was on her own.
>
>And now what we know of lions is
>The hunter is the lioness.
>She'll not be killed by beauty,
>She'd rather be alone.

3.11

(Valmont enters in a flurry, shouting as he seeks the marquise.)

VALMONT:
>I've won! I've won!
>The curtain's fallen!
>The game is through!
>I'm free now, madame!
>
>*(Finding her in the dressing room)*
>That haughty woman's been broken.
>In the end she proved untrue.

MARQUISE:
>*(Scandalized by the intrusion, and dismissing Victoire)*
>Did you believe she'd do otherwise?
>You've raised her far too high.
>She's no greater mystery than anyone else,
>You must now realize.

VALMONT:
>Perhaps, though different in some ways.
>The ecstasy was so complete, so pure,
>Nothing like I've known before...
>Anyway...

Now you have a debt to pay,
A debt you must afford.

MARQUISE:
"When love first comes,
It comes as a surprise,
And often unidentified as love at all."

VALMONT: What?

MARQUISE: Your words, vicomte!

The heart pounds,
The hands shake,
The tongue trips,
And tries to catch up.

VALMONT: Don't be ridiculous!

MARQUISE:
Admit it! You love her!
"Like nothing you ever have known!"

I don't want to interfere!
Love so strong should persevere!

VALMONT:
You can't think she compares to you,
Between you two there's no contest!

MARQUISE:
Be that as it may,
I won't belittle myself to play
The second role to anyone,
So I must declare our bargain null and void.

VALMONT:
You cannot.

MARQUISE:
I can and will,
Until you have been cured of this
Obscene malignancy you don't call love!
I do this for the both of us.

VALMONT: You can't be serious.

MARQUISE:
   Oh, but I am.
   And besides,
   I've someone new to keep me occupied.

VALMONT: You've taken another lover?

MARQUISE: Perhaps. You aren't the only one who needs a little adventure now and then. Oh, vicomte, don't think that I'm doing this out of spite. We both are free to explore our own individual ventures.

(Contemplative)
So much has changed in so short a time....

(Biting, resolved)
I think you should go back to the tender embraces of your angel.

VALMONT:
   I don't understand.
   Why all this jealousy?
   I thought you would be pleased...

MARQUISE:
   I'm beginning to see there's so much
   You do not understand of me.

VALMONT: Well, that's not my fault...

MARQUISE: *(Suddenly intolerant)*
I'm tired, vicomte. Leave me.

VALMONT:
   This isn't through.

MARQUISE:
   You're right, that's true.
   I will write you soon.

(She returns to sit at her mirror. Valmont hesitates, about to say something else, then decides better of it. He leaves without a kiss or bow. The marquise sits quietly.)

So now what we know of lions is
The hunter is the lioness.
She'll not be killed by beauty,
She'd rather be alone.

(She gazes at her reflection, deliberately raising her chin emphasizing nobility. Her mood pensive, dangerous. Lights fade.)

3.12

The Château Rosemonde. Volanges sits on the terrace, fanning herself and sipping something cool. Cécile comes out from the château with her shawl in hand.

VOLANGES:
You're up awfully late this morning.

CÉCILE:
I've been feeling ill.
My stomach was upset all night.

VOLANGES:
Perhaps you should return to bed.

CÉCILE: Maman, you worry about me too much.

VOLANGES: At least have something to eat.

CÉCILE: I'm not hungry right now. I'm going to take a short walk.

VOLANGES: Perhaps I'll join you...

CÉCILE:
I'm not a child!
When will you learn to trust me?

VOLANGES:
You're still my child.

CÉCILE:
I no longer need a chaperone
To follow everywhere I go.
I'm engaged —
(Flipping on her shawl, pointedly)
At least you've told me so.

(Cécile exits. Volanges sits, baffled, fluttering her fan.)

3.13
MOTHERHOOD

VOLANGES:
   What did I do?
   What did I say?
   It seems these days,
   Every little issue is a battle.
   And though I hate to say it,
   It's one I fear I'm losing.
   Please, would someone tell me how to handle...

Motherhood!
What a joy, what a ride!
Though it's true and it's tried,
There's no challenge like raising a daughter.

Motherhood!
It's a dream coming true,
Yes, a nightmare where you
Are the lamb being led to the slaughter!

All my years of living
Never prepared me for this.
This sweet, unforgiving,
Purgatorial bliss!

Motherhood!
No one told me how to handle motherhood.
No one could prepare me for the worst.
Once, I too was young,
My life had just begun,
But then I wed and there in bed
I caught the fam'ly curse.
Quickly caged at center stage,
Completely unrehearsed.

Motherhood!
Nothing could be more perplexing, motherhood!
Every choice you face has twenty sides.
And they should provide
A manual or a guide
That tells you firm in simple terms
The way to raise a child.
What things to buy,
What tricks they try
That leave you so beguiled.

Why they want one thing
And then want another.
Well, what is a mother to do?
If I were another,
I'd not be a mother,
No, I'd be a daughter too.

Children have it easy!
We hand them the world on a platter.
That doesn't matter!
You can give them the moon,
The sky as their stage,
Then so matter-of-factly
They turn out exactly
The way that you were at their age!

You rant and you rage,
You pant and you gauge,
And try to assuage,
While making a list
Of all that you've missed,
And counting the gray
That triples each day,
And knowing you're showing
The signs of your age!

(VOLANGES):
So how do you cope
Without losing hope?
She's getting too old
To do what she's told
(Or maybe too young).
Be that as it may,
She's slipping away.
And here comes the day
That you no longer pray for,
That terrible day
When she's finally engaged!

That will be a day...
(With sudden realization)
When you can relax...
Free from the axe...
(Picking up her drink)
Take a drink!
Have another!
What more could they ask?
You've weathered the task
Of being a mother!

(She empties her glass.)

3.14
CORRESPONDENCES 2

A split scene. Dançeny sits on his bed, writing a letter to Cécile. In her bed at Rosemonde's, Cécile reads the letter to Valmont, who is in bed beside her.

DANÇENY:
Dear Cécile,
Though we still are apart from each other,
A friendship has helped ease the pain.
Madame de Merteuil
Has been patient and listens,
And smiles when I mention your name.

(The marquise rises up beside him in bed, stroking his hair.)

My life is fulfilled with such sweetness.
I give thanks for both friendship and love.
And I see a time soon
When at last we're united,
Together, that's how we'll remain.

(As the letter ends, both Cécile and Dançeny are pulled into the arms of their respective lovers, the letters discarded. Lights fade on them and rise on Tourvel, and on Rosemonde, to whom she writes.)

TOURVEL:
So it goes, dearest friend,
I'm resolved to love him.
It's all that brings me pleasure
When my heart's most torn.

I've broken with my husband,
Made confession.
I know God forgives,
I won't be foresworn.

(The lights fade on Tourvel and Rosemonde, and rise back on Cécile's room, where Valmont now sits alone at the foot of the bed.)

VALMONT:
I am writing this letter,
Madame, to inform you,
My time with Cécile's at an end.
What she suffered last evening
Has nearly destroyed her...
I was once more instructing her when...

(Cécile rises up behind Valmont as the lights change to indicate a flashback. She puts her arms around his neck, singing into his ear.)

CÉCILE:
What a silly thing!
People fret too much.
We're given hands to feel and touch
Everywhere...

(CÉCILE):
(Sitting back)
Look at me sitting here,
I can be anyone's dream!
A breath, a kiss, one more caress...
I'm nothing and all that I seem.

VALMONT:
(Pulling her to him)
You at last have blossomed,
The world is awaiting your word!

CÉCILE:
If that is the case,
Lets not speak at all.
The best things in life are...

(Cécile cries out, doubling over in pain.)

VALMONT: Cécile, what's the matter?

CÉCILE: I'm... hurting, I... Help me!

(Intense red lighting as she cries out again, clasping her stomach. They freeze. There is a soft fade and the lights rise on the marquise reading Valmont's letter. A moment, and then we hear Valmont. The lights gradually come up on him through the remainder of his letter.)

VALMONT:
No one had known
That the girl had been several weeks pregnant.
No one will know,
I took measures to keep it a secret.
As for Cécile,
She's returning at long last to Paris.
Somehow, I feel
She's no longer the girl that she was.

MARQUISE:
>Dear Vicomte,
>I grow tired of your endless prattling,
>Your boasts and bravados grow old.
>You are tainted with softness,
>You're weakness is rattling,
>You're a sight I can barely behold.

(Valmont moves to join the marquise.)

>So what if the girl has been broken?
>So what if she's never the same?
>To the flames with compassion,
>Damn sympathies rationed
>To those who have lost to the game.

3.15
A Story

MARQUISE: You've played your part well in this matter, vicomte. Cécile is ruined to Gercourt. And, if we choose to let her miscarriage be known, it will be no great effort to do so.

VALMONT: Oh, enough of this. You did not invite me here tonight to speak of Cécile.

MARQUISE: True. To be honest, I have lost all interest in the girl.

>No, vicomte.
>It is you I wish to discuss,
>You who need guidance now.
>So heed me well,
>For I too have a story to tell.

(She claps her hands. Victoire appears in a foppish parody of a man that obviously resembles Valmont. Victoire plays out the marquise's story, treating the marquise as the object of her affection.)

>A man, like you, I knew
>Became entangled with a woman,
>Spurning all his friends
>And former lovers for this prude.

(MARQUISE):
   He was in danger of becoming
   Quite the laughing stock, you see.
   Though shackled by this woman,
   He bragged that he was free.

   At times he would grow lucid
   And perceive his sorry state,
   But then closed his eyes to danger,
   He answered all his friends
   Who tried to save him from his fate:

VICTOIRE:
   "It's not my fault!"

MARQUISE:
   That's what he shouted.

VICTOIRE:
   "It's not my fault!"

MARQUISE:
   As he would tout,
   "Well, any day I could leave!"
   He couldn't leave,
   He was trapped, you see.

   But a friend of his was wise,
   And she gave to him a letter
   Which explained how he could break the chains
   Which now were choking him.

   She bade him stage a meeting
   With the woman he'd defy,
   And to tell her he was leaving,
   And answer every protest
   That she gave with this reply:

VICTOIRE:
   It's not my fault,

MARQUISE:
   If this seems sordid.

VICTOIRE:
It's not my fault,

MARQUISE:
If I am bored.

VICTOIRE / MARQUISE:
It's just the way that things are.

VICTOIRE:
It's not my fault!

MARQUISE:
I love another.

VICTOIRE:
It's not my fault!

MARQUISE:
If she insists I give you up,
Then I must!

(Breaking the parody, rounding on Valmont)
That is the price to be paid for your sins.
Sacrifice one and the other you win.
Don't wait too long,
Or both you will lose.
It's up to you now.
Which one will you choose?

(Lights down)

3.16

The Château Volanges. Cécile's room and the hallway outside. A nurse attends to Cécile, who is at her desk, staring blankly into space.

NURSE: You haven't touched your supper. Goodness child, you'll make yourself ill! Well, is there anything more I can get for you? No, I don't suppose there is. Try and get some rest.

(The nurse exits into the hallway, where Volanges anxiously awaits.)

VOLANGES: Well? What is it? What's wrong with her?

NURSE: Nothing I can help, that's for certain. Medicine can do wonders, but the greatest doctor alive has yet to find a cure for a broken heart.

VOLANGES: A broken... What can I do?

NURSE: Just speak to her gently, and don't expect too much too soon. And getting a little food in her wouldn't hurt nothing, either.

VOLANGES: Thank you.

(The nurse exits. Volanges stands at Cécile's doorway, uncertain.)

3.17
SPEAK GENTLY

VOLANGES:
  Speak gently!
  Gentle words, is that the only cure?
  What can words do when she's
  Past the time for listening?
  Words are nothing.
  Words are useless in a truthless world!

> **(VOLANGES):**
>   Still I'll speak gently,
>   And try to understand.
>   I was young once, too!
>   The things I've seen
>   Were real to me then.
>
> **CÉCILE:**
> *(Alone in her room)*
>   Maman, I'm so unhappy.
>   Please try to understand.
>   If you only knew...
>   The things I've seen,
>   Are real to me now...

VOLANGES:
  Speak gently...
  Speak gently...
  Speak gently...
  Or don't speak at all.

CÉCILE:
  Maman, it isn't easy.
  I'm trying to be strong.
  But in order to be
  I mustn't speak at all.

(Volanges enters Cécile's room and both hear each other's last words. There is an awkward pause.)

VOLANGES: You're not hungry?

(A pause)
Cécile, I just want you to know...

CÉCILE: I do know, maman. I do. It just...

VOLANGES: ...doesn't matter. I was the same way at your age.

(Volanges strokes Cécile's hair without a response. She starts to go, but Cécile reaches out, tentatively at first, then hugs her mother fiercely.)

CÉCILE: Oh, Maman!

VOLANGES: Shhhh! Everything will be all right.

CÉCILE: Maman, I love you.

VOLANGES: *(Bending down to kiss her daughter's forehead)*
And I love you. With all my heart, I do.

(Volanges leaves, shutting the door gently behind her. In the hall outside, she wipes her tears.)

  Speak gently? No,
  Best not to speak at all.

(Volanges exits.)

3.18
REPRISE: THE GAME

CÉCILE:
If only I'd seen the ending,
If only I'd thought it through,
If only I'd been more careful,
I'd be with him...

Love is just a game,
But like the rain that falls,
It's cold and its dark
To a heart that would heed its call.

Once, I thought it'd last,
But now I'm past the game.
Now, tell me how
Did I ever want to be what I became?

(She cries into her hands as the lights fade.)

3.19
IT'S NOT MY FAULT

A Paris apartment, the current residence of Mme. de Tourvel. At rise, Tourvel sits, cheerfully awaiting the arrival of Valmont. He enters. He is quiet, his mood unreadable. Tourvel rushes to embrace him.

TOURVEL:
At last!
I knew that you were near.
Is it strange?
Do you think that my heart
Can tell when you are here?

My love, I hope that you are happy,
I want that most of all.
Tell me what you're feeling now.

VALMONT:
If only I felt anything,
But all I feel is boredom now.

TOURVEL: *(Confused, still cheerful)*
What?

VALMONT:
(Trying to begin)
It's not my fault...

TOURVEL: What do you mean?

VALMONT:
(Avoiding eye contact)
Well, what is love? It's tremulous at best.
A transitory feeling that's like all the rest.

It burns at the start,
But quickly grows colder.
Love is a thing
Not meant to grow older.
What can be done
When that is its nature?

(He tries again, but turns, and his eyes meet hers. He falters.)

It's not my...fault...

TOURVEL: Are you saying you don't love me?

VALMONT: I'm saying it doesn't matter, one way or the other.

We shared a dance made of one or two spins.
Faith in it lasting was our only sin.
Now we must part as all lovers do,
And if that seems cruel...

(VALMONT):
It's not my fault!
If this seems sordid,
It's not my fault!
If I am bored,
It's just the way that things are.

TOURVEL:
(Interjecting)
Why are you doing this?
What's happened to you?

TOURVEL: Do you love somebody else, is that it?

VALMONT: *(With gradually intensifying agitation)*
Yes, I do. I love another. A very jealous woman who now insists that I break from you. What choice do I have?

> (VALMONT):
> It's not my fault!
> I love another.
> It's not my fault!
> If she insists I give you up,
> Then I must.
>
> TOURVEL:
> *(Interjecting)*
> Stop this!
> I don't believe you!

TOURVEL:
> Is this what you are?
> Was I really so blind?
> I was warned,
> Did I choose not to hear?
> I should have listened.

VALMONT: Yes, you should have listened to Madame de Volanges' warnings. She knows me very well.

TOURVEL: How do you know...

VALMONT: I read your letters.

> I planned every detail, every move,
> For the easiest ones to deceive
> Are those who believe.
> But now let us face the truth:
>
> If your virtue isn't perfect,
> I am not the one to blame.
> It's not at all my fault!

TOURVEL:
(Taking hold of his shirt)
This can't be true.
Please say it's not!
Please take me in your arms...

VALMONT:
I didn't force you.
It's not my fault!
Madame, of course!
One final fling for good-bye!

(She strikes him, pushes him away.)

TOURVEL:
Get out of here!
You've played your game, so go!
You have your victory,
Go tell the world!
They all should know.
Leave me here!

(He hesitates, reaches for her. She pulls away.)

For God's sake, leave me!

(Valmont rushes from the room. Tourvel collapses.)

3.20
SOLILOQUY

The scene shifts to follow him out. He reels against a wall, seemingly in pain. He looks back the way he came, then defiantly shakes his feelings off.

VALMONT:
I've every reason to rejoice!
If I'm a fiend, then that's my choice!
I should be laughing,
Why do I want to scream?

Why should I feel so alone?
Why do I feel so afraid?
And why should I feel love?

(VALMONT):
>So the lesson is learned...
>And she loves me in turn!
>I hate her more for loving me!
>And I'll hold her again...
>No more.
>
>But I am free!
>And lost to everything I know.
>Where am I to go?
>Tell me who I am now,
>I no longer know
>Who I am, why I am, what I am,
>Where to go!
>
>If there's one who can tell,
>It's the one who has brought this on me!

(He rushes off.)

3.21
PROMISE ME ANYTHING

The scene shifts back to Tourvel, who, now alone, seems strangely calm.

TOURVEL:
>Promise me anything,
>But when it comes time to leave me,
>Keep for me only this vow:
>Hold me until I see clearly
>My present illusions,
>Delusions of what we are now.
>
>Promise me little things.
>Don't spin me tales of undying love.
>Make me no wishes come true.
>Just hold me close, let me dream of
>A world where no bane crowds,
>Where rain clouds will vanish on queue.
>
>And if we falter on the way,
>Or lose the sight of shore,
>We'll have each other for those days
>When life won't give us more.

And if there ever comes a time
When we regret the choice we've made,
Look deep into my eyes to find
A ghost of yesterday.

Promise me many things.
When you have found someone new,
And you see she is ready to fall...
Hold her, and kiss her, and love her true!
But don't promise her anything,
Anything at all!

3.22

(TOURVEL):
When we find feelings fail,
We spend seasons running from ourselves...

(Tourvel collapses, suddenly ill. As Julie rushes to help her mistress, the lights fade.)

3.23

The rumbling of another storm can be heard, culminating in a flash of lightning, which illuminates the marquise, once again at her vanity in the dressing room. The door to her boudoir is closed, the room itself concealed in shadow. She sits still as a statue, lost in contemplation. Another lightning flash, and Valmont is suddenly behind her. Their eye's meet in the mirror, and for the first moments of their conversation, they address each other's reflections.

VALMONT: How does the story end?

MARQUISE: What?

VALMONT: Your story, the one with your friend. How does it end?

MARQUISE: The ending has yet to be written.

(Valmont places his hands on her shoulders, caressing them. A smile plays across her lips. She allows her eyes to close, enjoying his touch, but not giving over to it.)

VALMONT:
  I have followed the course of your tale.
  Madame de Tourvel knows the sad lies of love,
  And the truth of betrayal.
  The ending is in place,
  I'm here now to receive my just reward.

(He continues to caress her. She gives in a bit more, places one of her hands over his and guides it to her lips.)

MARQUISE:
  Valmont, you've surpassed expectations.

VALMONT:
  Of course there is one thing
  That could prove a still greater challenge:
  The challenge of winning her back.
  To think that I could win her back...

(The sensuous mood is abruptly broken. The marquise opens her eyes.)

MARQUISE: Do you really believe that?

VALMONT: Yes.

MARQUISE: *(Standing suddenly, moving away from him)*
Impossible.

VALMONT: Why?

MARQUISE:
  Because she's been inflicted
  With the deadliest of ills.
  When a woman strikes another woman
  Usually she kills.
  I've turned your love to poison
  Of which she has had her fill.

VALMONT:
  Your jealousy's speaking,
  You're trying to claim what's mine!
  I won by myself,
  Without you and all your designs.

MARQUISE:
I don't need a victory over her.
She's as witless as your classic ingénue.
Oh, but I do claim my victory over you!

You placed me beneath her,
You made her my rival,
You loved her,
But thanks to your need for denial,
To turn you against her
Proved no great a trial.
You'd sell away your soul for pride!

VALMONT:
Don't bore me to death with your cleverness.
I'm not here to speak about love,
I'm sick of that word!
I've come here to claim what is mine,
I think that I've earned it!

(Valmont moves in the direction of her boudoir.)

MARQUISE: Where are you going?

VALMONT: To bed, of course. I suggest you join me.

MARQUISE: Stop it, Valmont! Get out of here. No!

(Valmont throws open the doors to the marquise's boudoir, where the lights rise, revealing Dançeny in the marquise's bed. He jumps up, startled. There is a moment of realization for all three.)

VALMONT:
(Rounding on Dançeny)
This is the thanks I get for helping you.
Insolent pranks, but still I'm helping you.
Let me be frank,
The girl we all thought you loved
Has returned to Paris at last.

DANÇENY: Cécile is back? How...

VALMONT:
   She has been ill,
   Did you know?
   Do you care?
   Did you think she would wait for this dalliance?
   Soon she returns to the convent,
   And this time for good!

MARQUISE: Stop it, vicomte.

DANÇENY: *(Stumbling out of bed, tripping on the sheets as he comes)*
No! I have to go to her. I have to see her.

MARQUISE: What?

DANÇENY:
   Madame, you must forgive me,
   Our time has been so charming
   And I hope that now and always
   We will remain the best of friends.
   But Cécile... She's back!
   I have to speak to her
   Before it is too late!

VALMONT:
   (Gathering up Dançeny's clothes, throwing them at him.)
   Here, take your clothes,
   Wipe your nose,
   And dispose of useless excuses.
   Don't waste my precious time!

Go!

(Dançeny bows awkwardly, fumbling with his clothes as he exits.)

   You played me a sorry fool for that oafish boy!

MARQUISE:
   That boy has greater stamina than you.

VALMONT:
   Well, you can be the judge when we're finished.
   (Indicating the bed)
   Would you prefer a change of linens?

MARQUISE:
You dare to give me orders in that condescending pitch?
You must have me mistaken for your sweet angelic bitch!
So scream, or beg, or pine away, you don't control my life.
What makes you think you have the right
to treat me like a wife?

You don't know what a challenge is.
You've had the easier road to take.
You make sport of hurting women,
I take pride in destroying a man.

So our nature is one.
We're the same, you and I.
But society makes a hero of you,
And me they would crucify!
If I can't make the rules,
I'll break them.
I've too much to lose not to win.
So this game's at an end.

VALMONT: I could ruin you so easily.

MARQUISE:
And I could do the same.

Stalemate, vicomte.

VALMONT:
You refuse to acknowledge what's true,
Once you've made up your mind.
But I'll try to be perfectly clear on this point.

MARQUISE: I doubt you can.

VALMONT:
Only one word,
I will be an enemy or lover.

MARQUISE: Do not make me choose.

VALMONT:
Yes or no. Win or lose.

MARQUISE:
There's no going back once I have chosen.

VALMONT:
No more protests to make.
I will stand for no objections,
And take any obstacles for
A declaration of war.

MARQUISE:
The choice is easy, then.

VALMONT: Good.

MARQUISE:
I choose war!

(They face each other, each one unmoving. There is a crash of lightning. Blackout.)

3.24
SALVE REGINA / THE VEIL IS TORN

From the darkness rise the somber voices of a choir of nuns singing at a distance, from off stage.

CHOIR:
Sálve, Regína,
Máter misericórdiae:
Víta, dulcédo,
Et spes nóstra, sálve.

(As the verse progresses, the stage lightens from black to shades of gray. Silhouettes of two nuns pass before the shadow of a bed, which sits center stage.)

Ad te clamámus,
Éxsules, fílii hévae.

(The stage lightens even more, the gray giving way to pale amber, and Tourvel can be seen in the bed, caught in the grips of a feverish sleep. Julie sits in a chair by the bed, also asleep.)

(CHOIR):
   Ad te suspirámus,
   Geméntes et fléntes
   In hac lacrimárum válle.

Eia ergo, advocáta nóstra,

TOURVEL:
   (Still asleep, dreaming)
   How could I not believe...
   How did I believe...
   Don't hold back the things you feel!
   Let me...
   Let me see you,
   Let me see you...
   No! No! ...

(Julie awakens at Tourvel's cry. She observes her mistress for a moment.)

CHOIR:
   Íllos túos misericórdes óculos
   Ad nos convérte.

(Julie goes to Tourvel dampens a cloth in a basin beside the bed, and takes Tourvel's hand.)

(CHOIR):
   Et Jésum, benedíctum frúctum véntris túi,

TOURVEL:
   The veil is torn,
   And happiness dies!
   Darkness...
   Darkness...
   Darkness all around me!

(Julie wipes Tourvel's forehead with the cloth.)

CHOIR:
Nóbis post hoc exsílium osténde.
O clémens:
O pía:

TOURVEL:
Here among the trees,
Among the seas of roses,
Darkness...
Darkness!

I'm again at ease....
Please...
Please...
Darkness everywhere!

TOURVEL: It is darkness that befits me...

CHOIR:
O dúlcis virgo María.

3.25

The lights on Julie and Tourvel dim as others rise to reveal the Mother Superior, Volanges, and Cécile talking as they approach Tourvel's door.

VOLANGES: How long has she been here?

MOTHER SUPERIOR: Three days. She came to us without an explanation. She asked to see her old room and, once she was there, she refused to leave. It's terrible. Her maid is with her now.

VOLANGES: I wish I had known sooner.

MOTHER SUPERIOR: *(Pausing at the door)*
She is extremely ill. Her mind comes in and out of delirium, her body in and out of fever....

TOURVEL:
(Suddenly awake)
No!
Valmont!
Let me die!

(Volanges rushes into the room, followed by the Mother Superior and Cécile. Julie looks helplessly up at them as she tries to calm her mistress.)

JULIE: Madame, please, you are safe!

TOURVEL:
No, can't you see him?
He's there, laughing at me!

(Seeing Volanges moving toward her)
Oh madame, my friend, you are here!
I do not deserve to see you again.
I am dying because I did not believe you.
I deserve this misery!

VOLANGES: No. You've only ever deserved happiness.

TOURVEL:
No, please,
It's too late for me.
Put out the light.
I belong in darkness.
Leave me...
Leave me...
Leave me in darkness.

(Tourvel lapses back into unconsciousness. Volanges is silent for a moment, overcome.)

VOLANGES: Madame de Rosemonde. She needs to know what has happened. They were like mother and daughter.

(Cécile reaches a hand out to her mother. Volanges takes it and holds it to her cheek.)

CÉCILE: How did this happen? What caused it?

VOLANGES: Oh, I know what caused it. I know who caused it. And if there is any justice in this world, then the Vicomte de Valmont will suffer as cruel a fate as that which he has inflicted upon this poor child.

(The lights fade.)

3.26
FINAL SCENE

A dim spot on a center stage platform. The marquise writes a letter.

MARQUISE:
There are crimes in this world
That cannot be forgiven.
I'm writing to tell you of one.
Oh my poor chevalier,
It's for you that I'm grieving,
For some things cannot be undone.

The Vicomte de Valmont has betrayed you!
He's made mockery of all you hold dear.
In your place he has taken
Cécile for his lover,
Replacing her laughter with fear.

(As she continues, similar spots come up, down right and down left, on Valmont and Dançeny, who enter, followed by their respective valets, Azalon and Luc, each of whom carries a long case under his arm. Azalon also carries a second box, a small chest of sorts. Valmont and Dançeny stand apart, facing the audience. Once in position, the two Valets place their boxes on the ground.)

Here is the proof!
I'm enclosing his treacherous letter.
Therein the truth
Of this monster is yours to unfetter.
Think of Cécile,
Whom he made his unwitting abettor.
How she must feel!
And what's left to be done...

DANÇENY:
...I will do.

(Azalon takes Valmont's coat. Luc, Dançeny's cape, and the ornamental sabers worn daily, are also removed from their waists. As the scene shifts, the spot on the marquise slowly fades to black.)

VALMONT:
I just want this madness to end.
Why wish for a thing I can't have?

LUC:
(To Dançeny)
You still can call this whole thing off,
I wish you would.

DANÇENY:
I can't!
Not when I've failed so many times.
I can't give in,
Not when there's a chance for a nobler ending.

AZALON:
(To Valmont)
The boy is doomed to fail
Against a swordsman such as you.
Let's not pretend.
There's not a chance for him of winning.

VALMONT:
(Rolling back his sleeves)
For better or for worse,
This has to end.

(The scene opens, revealing the street, which begins to fill with gathering spectators.)

MAN 1:
What is the commotion?

MAN 2:
Do you have a notion?

MAN 3:
Heard the news just yesterday.
They say the chevalier
Has made the challenge.

WOMAN 1:
So then, are they dueling?

MAN 4:
God, but this is grueling!

WOMAN 2, 3:
Sad this has to be,
It's quite disturbing!

(PLUS) MAN 1, 4:
This I simply have to see!

ALL SPECTATORS:
I'll wager six or seven,
The filling straight from my tooth.

MAN 4:
Valmont's the far better swordsman.

OLDER MAN:
But the chevalier has his youth.

(Azalon and Luc are serving as their masters' witnesses. They move somberly to confer with each other. When they meet, Luc holds out a hand to shake, but Azalon folds his arms. In pantomime, they begin determining the rules. The spectators continue to gather.)

MAN 3:
Both of 'em look sickly.

OLD WOMAN:
Get it over quickly!

MAN 1:
Hope they do it soon, I say!
I haven't got all day.
Let's see some action!

WOMAN 4:
My feet are getting muddy.

MAN 2:
This had best be bloody!

ALL WOMEN:
Take ten paces, turn around,
Let's hear the sound of swords a-clashing!

ALL MEN:
Flashing points of steel
Anointed now in crimson!

WOMAN 3:
(To Man 3)
Send someone to fetch a priest!

MAN 3:
I am a priest!

SPECTATORS:
How they must feel,
Knowing one may have seen his last morning.
One seems afraid,
And the other seems lost to our warning.
They made the choice,
So we needn't go on like we're mourning.

VALMONT:
How can I do anything,
When all I can think of is her?

(Azalon and Luc separate, returning to their masters. They finish their preparations by issuing gloves, and selecting swords from the long cases, testing the weight and balance of each.)

DANÇENY:
If only I had seen this before,
I'd not have made the choices I made.
The moments fade away...
I've seen how sweet my life can be...
I don't want to die!

VALMONT:
If only I could alter the past,
But pride has led me to this moment.
I've seen how sweet my life can be...
But how can I live?

AZALON / LUC: *(Handing the swords to their respective masters)*
Monsieur, your sword.

3.27
THE DUEL

(The swords are taken up. Dançeny and Valmont face each other. Lights rise on Tourvel's bed at the convent, where Volanges, Cécile, and Julie still attend their ailing friend. Azalon picks up the small chest, and both valets stand aside and wait, as the duel begins. Valmont is obviously the better swordsman. Dançeny swings and parries clumsily. The spectators make intermittent comments on the battle. Then Tourvel, delirious, calls from her bed.)

TOURVEL:
...And if we falter on the way...

(Valmont turns from the battle, in response to the ghostly whisper. Dançeny leaps after him. Valmont blocks the blow without a glance, then presses after Dançeny, angered by the interruption. Valmont beats Dançeny down. Luc comes to his master's aid, as Valmont raises his head to the sky to hear Tourvel.)

Oh my love, my life, you're here again!
Let me breathe again the summer in your hair.
Take my hand, let all this madness disappear.
Let this world of sorrow fade into the air.

VALMONT:
There is only one way...
Only one way to be happy...

TOURVEL:
Only one way to be happy...

(Valmont turns, his sword ready, as Dançeny rises.)

TOURVEL:
(Climbing out of bed, becoming more agitated)
What are you doing?
What bonds are you seeking to break?

VALMONT:
Only one way...

TOURVEL:
Stay with me!
Don't abandon me again!

VALMONT:
Only one way to end this!

(Dançeny charges Valmont.)

TOURVEL:
(Shouting, horrified)
Dear God!
Leave me!

(Valmont, at the last moment, lowers his guard, is run through, and falls into Dançeny, as Tourvel falls into Volanges' arms. Dançeny lowers him to the ground, and steps back in terror. Azalon, still carrying the chest, rushes to them, quickly puts the chest down, and reaches for Valmont, supporting him. Luc approaches, holding Dançeny's cape.)

3.28

(The spectators have fallen silent. Gradually, as Valmont speaks, a few of them draw nearer, gathering around.)

VALMONT:
(Addressing Dançeny)
Please, there is so much to say,
It's important you listen.
I cannot explain now my actions,
But know the Marquise de Merteuil
Is no friend to you.
She has betrayed you as surely as I.

She is the one pulling both of our strings,
She and I played a dangerous game.
She's equaled my evil in every way,
Now I too have been caught in her flame.

You have cause to suspect what I say,
So I'm giving you these...
(Reaching for the chest, pushing it to Dançeny.)
Read the truths you deserve,
You may pass them along.

(Kneeling, Dançeny opens the chest, reaches in and pulls out a handful of letters. Astonished, he shuffles them through his hands, as Valmont continues.)

(VALMONT): Believe me, I am not your enemy.

(To the gathered crowd)
I order you all to treat this gentleman with the respect that is owed him. He has earned it.

(Then, to Dançeny)
Now, I beg one favor from you...

DANÇENY: Yes?

VALMONT:
    Madame de Tourvel has fallen ill,
    You must go find her.
    Tell her that I'm gone,
    And tell her that I loved her until the end.
    I was blind to hurt her as I did.
    Tell her death is nothing,
    Death is welcome now.
    Tell her, as my eyes close one last time.

(Dançeny stands up, stunned, looking at the letters in his hands.)

Go now.

(Suddenly, Dançeny passes several of the letters to some of the spectators, picks up the chest, grabs his cape from Luc, and leaves for the convent. He passes behind the convent, and arrives on the far side, followed by Luc. They are greeted by a nun, who escorts only Dançeny to Tourvel.)

3.29
WHEN SILENCE REIGNS

(Dançeny sits down at Tourvel's bedside, his back to the audience. Meanwhile, in the street, some spectators still remain, but the lighting has narrowed on Valmont.)

VALMONT:
    There are no words now,
    Silence alone can tell the world
    The story of our love.
    It holds me still now.
    Strange how I see at last
    The wonders of this life.

Since nothing lasts forever,
Then my love can never die,
For everything at last
Gives way to silence.

TOURVEL: *(Turning to Dançeny, who has been speaking to her)*
Enough. I know enough.

(To everyone)
Please, leave me now.

(Dançeny stands and bows. He and Cécile exchange a look, and Cécile looks away. Dançeny exits. Volanges makes a move, a plea, but Tourvel stops her with a shake of her head. Volanges, Cécile, and Julie all exit, leaving Tourvel alone.)

(TOURVEL):
There are no words now.
Silence speaks every word of love
I ever hoped to say.
My heart grows still now.
Somehow, love is growing
Stronger as it fades.

Though nothing lasts forever,
There are truths that never change...

VALMONT:
There are no more regrets.
No more prayers to be said.
And very soon my light will fade...
But now you're standing here before me...

And although nothing lasts forever,
There are truths that never change....

TOURVEL:
...and love alone remains
When silence reigns.

(They die. Volanges and Cécile return to Tourvel's room with Father Anselme. They discover that she has died. Azalon closes Valmont's eyes. Father Anselme closes Tourvel's, makes the sign of the cross, and quietly begins giving her the last rights. In tears, Volanges and Cécile embrace each other. With the help of some of the remaining spectators,

Valmont's body is lifted from the street and carried off, and the convent fades. As they move away, the marquise is revealed alone at center, seated with a letter. Discovering the news of the duel, her hand quickly moves to her mouth in alarm as she reads. Her shock then turns to an expression of pensive dread, and her eyes forget the letter. A line of figures, each holding one of the marquise's letters, appears behind her. As the music ends, the letters are raised defiantly over their heads or in the direction of the marquise.)

Recording Credits

DANGEROUS LIAISONS Complete Original Concept
Melpomene Records, CD: 74099
Malcolm Caluori, executive producer / project coordinator

Recorded in June and August 2003, and February 2004. Recording released to the public 13 December 2011 with these additional recording and chorus credits:

Music Orchestrated and Directed by Malcolm Caluori

Casting: Malcolm Caluori and Johnathan Daniel Steppe
Technical Consulting: Gemini
Recording Engineer, Editor, Sound Design: Malcolm Caluori
Mixed at Melpomene Studios, Atlanta

Special thanks to: Susan V. Booth, Brian Mcleod,
Carmen Yamamoto, Michael Wolf, Andy Wathen,
and Sharon Notari

Azalon (Valet to Valmont)	Kevin Tucker
Le Commandeur	Tad Wilson
Gentleman Guest	Kevin Tucker
Le Comte de Gercourt	Steve Benton
Julie (Maid to Tourvel)	Wendy Kremer
M. de LeCroix	Tony Cimafranca
M. et Mme. LaPierre	Shealtiel Y'Israel, Teresa Williams
Luc (Valet to Dançeny)	Malcolm Caluori
Le Marquis de Merteuil	Johnathan Daniel Steppe
Mother of the Marquise	Denise Arribas
Mother Superior	Minnie Tee
Major Domo (to Rosemonde)	Malcolm Caluori
Major Domo (to Volanges)	Ron Tuck
Nurse	Deborah Levey
Opera Tenor	Malcolm Caluori
Priest	John Cawthon
Shoemaker	Will Simson
Tax Collector	John Jones
Victoire (Maid to Merteuil)	Wendy Arthur Balance
Young Marquise de Merteuil	Sage Notari

Cantor	Myfanwy Callahan
Deaf Old Man	John Cawthon
Effeminate Man	Johnathan Daniel Steppe
Friend (to Volanges)	Wendy Arthur Ballance
Man I	Tad Wilson
Man II	Brandon Kirby
Man III	Ken Anderson
Man IV	Steve Benton
Older Man	John Cawthon
Two Men	Ron Tuck, David Van Mersbergen
Woman I	Melissa Miller
Woman II	Sherri Von Hagel
Woman III	Teresa Williams
Woman IV	Jamila Sampson
Young Couple	Myfanwy Callahan, Brandon Kirby

GOSSIPS:

Giddy Woman	Tami Collup Scheinman
Old Woman	Kristie McCarthy
Young Prude	Melissa Peters

HUNTERS:
Brandon Kirby, Zandro Zaragoza, Ken Anderson, John Jones

SOCIALITES:
Heidi Bevill, Wendy Arthur Ballance, Deborah Levey,
Tony Cimafranca, Shealtiel Y'Israel, Will Simson

YOUNG GIRLS:
Liz Gordon, Meredith Mullins, Pilar Rehert

CHORUS ENSEMBLE:

Denise Arribas, Wendy Arthur Balance, Steve Benton,
Heidi Bevill, Myfanwy Callahan, John Cawthon, Ron Chenoweth,
Tony Cimafranca, Robin Fennell, Megan Hodge, John Jones,
Brandon Kirby, Wendy Kremer, Deborah Levey,
Kristie McCarthy, Melissa Miller, Melissa Peters,
Jamila Sampson, Tami Collup Scheinman, Will Simson,
Johnathan Daniel Steppe, Ron Tuck, Kevin Tucker,
David Van Mersbergen, Sherri Von Hagel, Teresa Williams,
Shealtiel Y'Israel, Zandro Zaragoza

Photo © 2003 Devette Freeney

Maura Carey Neill and Malcolm Caluori

Dangerous Liaisons Complete Original Concept recording
and Official Selections piano/vocal songbook
also available at:

www.DangerousLiaisonsTheMusical.com

Explore the story, the music
and the recording online now

Also from Melpomene Music Publications

Killing Valmont

The Creation of Caluori and Steppe's *Dangerous Liaisons*
Process, Content and Innovations

By D. Hector Francis

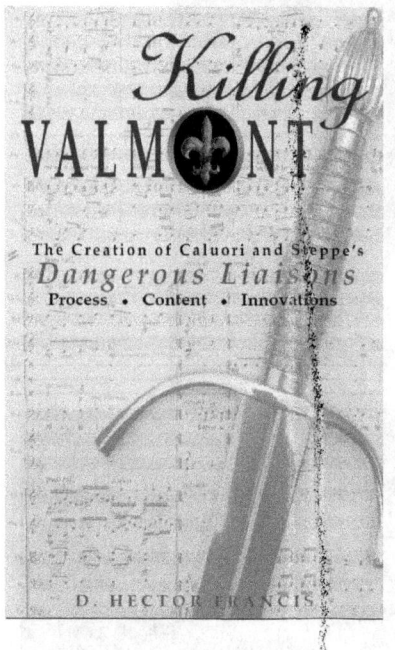

"I think even I have learned a few things about Dangerous Liaisons"

Malcolm Caluori

Get a rare view of musical drama from the inside out with an in-depth look at the ideas behind the work that dared to rethink the blending of music with drama.

The ultimate *Dangerous Liaisons* book for the dedicated theatre fan.

www.KillingValmont.com

www.ingramcontent.com/pod-product-compliance
Lightning Source LLC
Chambersburg PA
CBHW061641040426
42446CB00010B/1531